SOCIAL SECURITY
Disability Benefits

INITIAL FILING GUIDE 2019

Save up to $6,000 by filing your own application!

Written by
Jeffrey Herman, Esq.

A screen-by-screen guide on how to file an
initial application for disability benefits
all on your own!

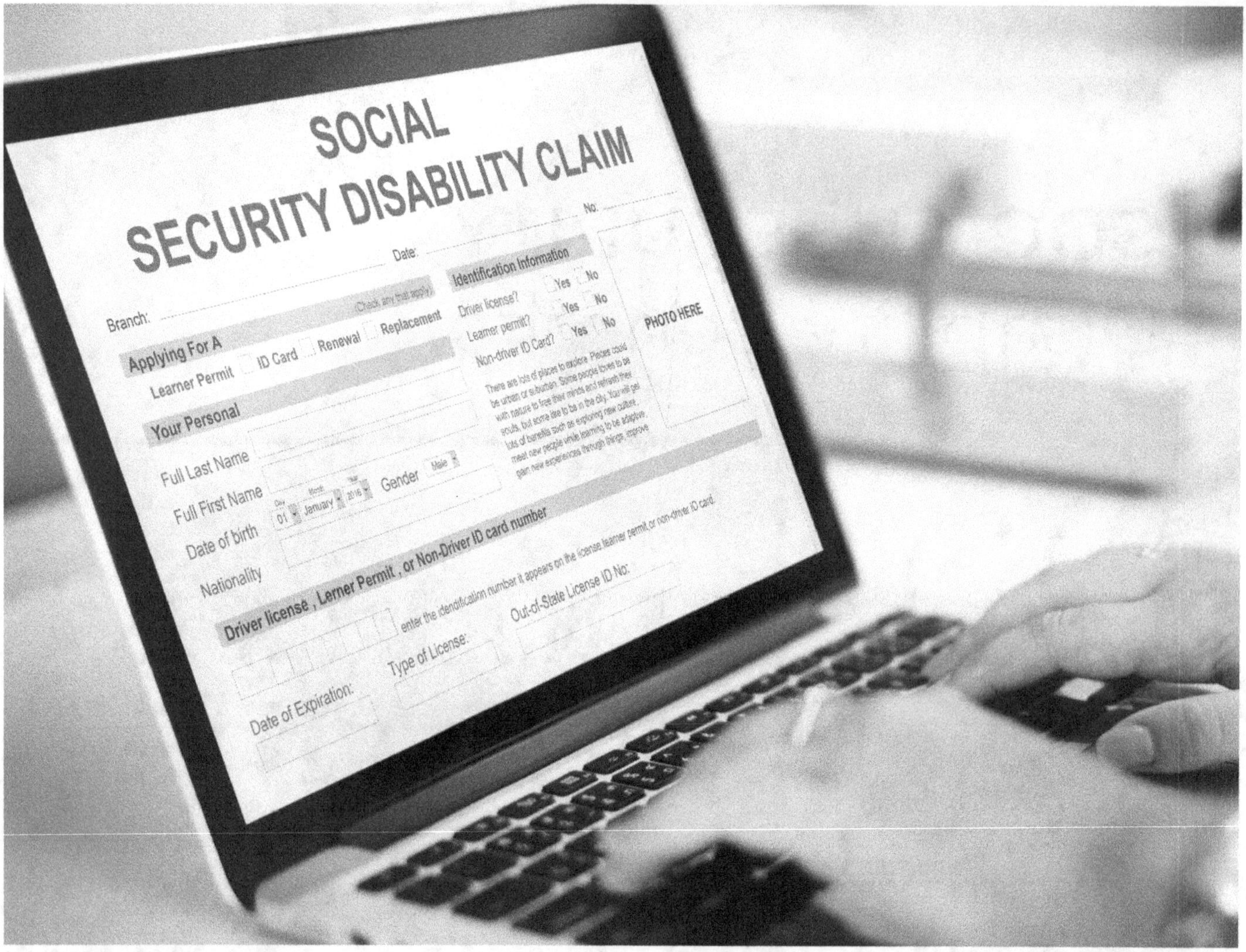

Filing your own Initial Application for Social Security Disability Insurance online
could save you up to $6,000!

(Yes, you read that correctly.)

I'm here to walk you through the filing process.

How can filing your own initial application online save you up to $6,000?

When you hire an attorney to represent your claim, the attorney's fee is 25% of your retroactive benefits (the back pay to which you're entitled). Federal law caps that fee at $6,000. You could save yourself this expense by filing your own initial application for Social Security Disability Insurance (SSDI) or Supplemental Security Income (SSI) benefits *without* the help of an attorney.

Be Forewarned

I'm sharing this information with you because you should always be armed with as much knowledge as possible before making any important decision.

Here's my warning to you: Don't get your hopes up too high. To be quite frank, it isn't easy to get an SSDI claim approved. In fact, less than 20% of disability claims are approved on initial review. An experienced attorney can sometimes tip the scales in your favor, and I highly recommend that you consider consulting with one if your initial application is denied.

Because attorneys know that initial applications are denied 4 out of 5 times, it's often better for you to file your own application online and seek assistance on appeal.

Note: When you see this icon in this eGuide, it means an important message about the SSDI claim process is on its way.

Note: When you see this ⚠ in this eGuide, it means a warning is headed your way.

A Brief Introduction

I've created this 2019 eGuide to help disabled people seize control of their lives by taking the first step in the notoriously lengthy and painstaking process of collecting SSDI benefits from the US government.

This eGuide offers step-by-step assistance for submitting your own application for SSDI or SSI. I've documented the entire process from start to finish. I've also highlighted certain key terms and posed questions meant to guide you through the process. This eGuide is peppered with useful tidbits that will help you prepare your application.

Working full-time in Social Security law has afforded me a glimpse into the lives of my clients, folks who suffer from a wide array of disabilities. Each person has a different story to tell, but the common thread in all the stories is struggle: medical struggle, emotional struggle, financial struggle. Knowing how far SSDI or SSI goes in relieving some of that suffering, nothing makes me happier than seeing a claim awarded to a deserving client. I hope that this eGuide will help folks see light at the end of the tunnel. As I write this, I'm 38 years old and in good health, but if I'm fortunate enough to live to 58, I might not be so healthy. If I were disabled and in need of SSDI, I would want an eGuide like this one to help me navigate the difficult application process.

My goal in writing this eGuide is simple: I want to explain the initial application process clearly so that applying on your own is manageable. I've tried to make this manual as convenient as possible, and I hope it makes your life a little easier. You have enough on your plate already, and I know a little help can go a long way. Let's get started!

Note: When you see this icon in this eGuide, it means you should expect an important message about the legal consequences of a question.

Table of Contents

Important Disclaimer	Pg. 4
Brief Introduction	Pg. 5
Table of Contents	Pg. 6
About the Author	Pg. 7
Some Fatherly Words	Pg. 8
Keep These Things in Mind	Pg. 9
How Disability Claims Are Analyzed	Pg. 10
Social Security Disability Vernacular (Common Acronyms)	Pg. 11
Social Security Disability Vernacular Cont. (Commonly Used Terms)	Pg. 12
Social Security Disability Vernacular Cont.	Pg. 13
Preliminary Test	Pg. 14
Initial Application Online Filing Checklist	Pg. 15
Create a "my Social Security" Account	Pgs. 16-20
Getting Started	Pgs. 21-27
Step 1 – Provide Background Information	Pgs. 28-49
Return to Your Saved Application	Pgs. 50-53
Step 1 – Provide Background Information (Review and Submit)	Pgs. 54-57
Step 2 – Provide Disability Information	Pgs. 58-86
Step 3 – Sign Medical Release	Pg. 87
Step 4 – Confirmation	Pg. 88
Congratulations	Pg. 89
What Happens Next?	Pg. 90
When Should You Consider Hiring an Attorney Representative?	Pg. 91

Important Disclaimer

Please note that while this eGuide has been drafted by an attorney, it does not constitute legal advice. Disability claims are like snowflakes: no two are alike. This eGuide contains general guidance only on how to complete an initial application for Social Security Disability Insurance (SSDI) benefits using the electronic filing system at www.ssa.gov. The tips provided in this eGuide may not apply to your unique set of circumstances.

Furthermore, no book or guide can ever replace the level of proficient representation you are entitled to when you enter an attorney/client relationship. In the area of Social Security law, an attorney/client relationship is only formed through a signed fee agreement. Your purchase or use of this eGuide does not create an attorney/client relationship between you and me.

To the best of my knowledge, this 2019 edition is the first of its kind. I have tried to provide a timely walkthrough of the online application process for disability benefits. It is important to note that the application process may be modified by SSA at any time and without advance notice. Regardless, the substance of the material is grounded in a core understanding of the Constitutional right that a disabled individual is entitled to.

Lastly, there are no guarantees that following this eGuide will result in an approval of your initial application.

About the Author

One Day, Two Births: Jeffrey Herman was born on September 11, 1980, in Long Island, New York. On the very day of Jeffrey's birth, his father, Stephen Herman, opened the doors to his own Social Security disability law practice, nestled in the courthouse district of Hempstead, New York.

Young, but Experienced: While Jeffrey was attending college in Queens 22 years later, Stephen offered his son a job in his firm. Jeffrey sat in on many of his father's initial consultations with Social Security disability clients. He witnessed firsthand how an attorney with more than 20 years of experience interviewed potential clients and assessed disability claims. Jeffrey also learned about the various procedural requirements, forms, and objective medical evidence required for approval of Social Security disability claims.

In 2013, Jeffrey followed in his father's footsteps and opened a practice of his own in Scottsdale, Arizona, where he now concentrates on SSDI claims. He holds a bachelor's degree in English, and he prides himself on his persuasive writing abilities.

> *"The key to overturning a wrongly denied disability claim is to write concise and persuasive briefs, which is something I do for each of my clients. In order to sway a judge, it's critical to use strong, clear language to explain why the decision to deny a claim should be reconsidered. I use a five-step sequential process that resonates with legal minds. I also use colorful and descriptive language to convey a client's pain, suffering, and physical limitations. My goal is to complement sound legal arguments with the human touch. I want both to persuade and to evoke empathy."*
>
> *- Jeffrey Herman*

Fun Fact: In addition to practicing Social Security disability law, Jeffrey is also an inventor who holds a patent on a unique napkin concept. The patent was issued on his 38th birthday.

Some Fatherly Words...

I was pleased and honored when my son Jeffrey asked me to contribute to his self-help tutorial for applying for Social Security disability benefits. Having practiced Social Security disability law since 1980, I have been able to impart to him much knowledge and practical advice on successfully representing a disability client. I believe that the cases are won in the preparation phase, by completing the Social Security forms accurately and fully and by getting medical and opinion evidence in a form most useful in a disability determination. My success rate of more than 80% testifies to the benefits of thorough preparation. My son's success to date is further confirmation.

In this self-help guide, Jeffrey lays the groundwork for a solid initial application, step by step, in easy-to-understand language. He also provides valuable tips on how to increase your chances of winning your case on initial application. Appeal times to a hearing before an ALJ run up to two years in many jurisdictions, so the advantage of being successful on initial application is obvious.

I will be retiring this year after 45 years of practicing law. One of the highlights of my career is the satisfaction of having many unfavorable decisions for disability benefits overturned, when people who have suffered long and hard with disabilities finally get the economic and medical benefits they so badly need. Those benefits often make dealing with a disability less burdensome. It is unfair that deserving claimants must often wait years to receive a benefit to which they are entitled.

I believe that Jeffrey Herman's self-help guide can assist persons to receive benefits sooner or to have a greater possibility of success on appeal.

Keep These Things in Mind

There Are 4 Steps to Filing

The initial filing process is broken into **4 Steps**. You must fully complete and submit each step in order to move on to the next one. These steps include Background Info, Disability Info, Medical Release, and Confirmation.

Once a step is finished, you won't be able to go back to change your responses. Before you begin, be prepared with the necessary information so you can fully and accurately complete each step.

No Need to File All at Once

Once you begin your initial application, you'll receive a **Record Locator Number**. You can use this "locator number" to return to your application at any time.

While there's no time limit for filing your application, your web browser may occasionally "time out" due to inactivity, and you'll need to log in using the location number to restore your progress.

Be Prepared and Take Your Time

Review our checklist for the information you'll need before you begin filing. Take your time in answering the questions. If you're not sure of an answer, you can always take a break to gather whatever information you need.

You Have Nothing to Fear

Some people worry that if their initial application isn't perfect, it will be immediately denied. That's simply not true. If you make an innocent mistake, it's not the end of the world. Oversights and errors are common, and you can usually correct them by calling or writing to a Social Security Administration (SSA) office.

Need Help?

If you get stuck on something, don't be afraid to send me an email! If you were kind enough to invest in this eGuide, I'll be happy to explain further a tricky question. In fact, your questions will make the 2020 version of this eGuide that much better for other applicants. I'll do my best to answer your questions as quickly as possible so you can keep moving through your application.

How Disability Claims Are Analyzed
The 5-Step Sequential Review Process

Note: Each step is reviewed in order. If a claim doesn't pass one of the steps, the claim is denied without continuing to any of the remaining steps.

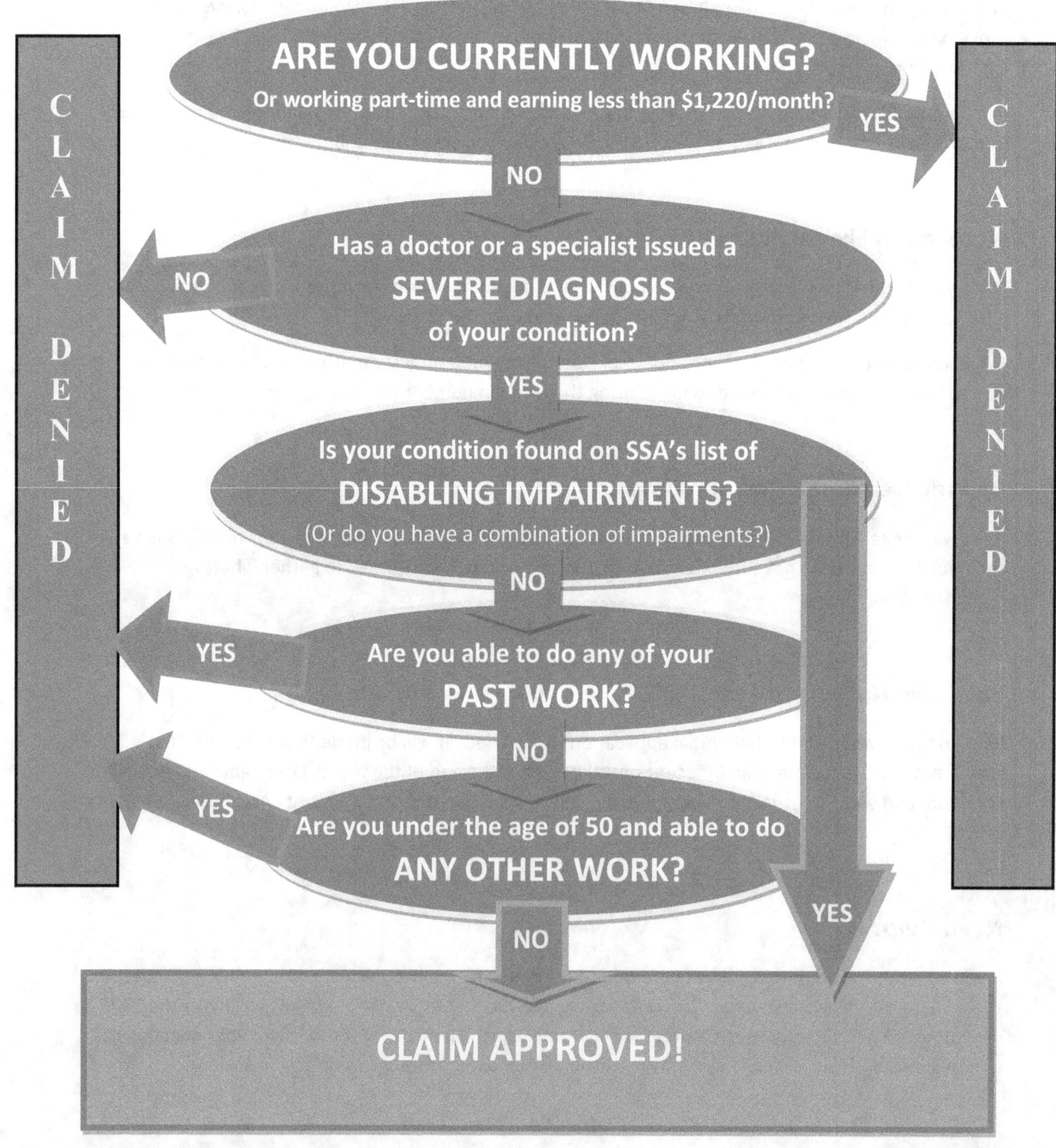

© 2019 Jeffrey Herman, Esq.   Ph: (844) 454-3762

Social Security Disability Vernacular

Common Acronyms

COLA – Cost of Living Adjustment
Social Security benefits and Supplemental Security Income (SSI) payments may be automatically increased each year to keep pace with increases in the cost of living (i.e., inflation).

DDS – Disability Determination Services
State agencies that are funded by the US government. Their purpose is to make disability findings for the Social Security Administration.

DOT – Dictionary of Occupation Titles
The D-O-T refers to a publication produced by the United States Department of Labor. The 1991 version of the D-O-T is still used extensively at SSA in litigation related to applications for Social Security disability benefits and Supplemental Security Income (SSI) for adult claimants.

FBR – Federal Benefit Rate
The federal benefit rate represents both the SSI income limit and the maximum federal monthly SSI payment.

FICA – Federal Insurance Contributions Act
The tax withheld from your salary or self-employment income that funds Social Security and Medicare.

RFC – Residual Functional Capacity
The amount of labor you can perform given your age, work history, and education, considering any physical or mental limitations caused by your disability(ies).

SGA – Substantial Gainful Activity
To be eligible for disability benefits, a person must be unable to engage in substantial gainful activity. The monthly SGA amount is $1,220 in 2019.

SSA – Social Security Administration
The government body that reviews disability claims and processes Social Security payments.

SSDI or SSD – Social Security Disability Insurance (Title II Benefits)
Monthly benefits that you will receive from SSA if your disability claim is approved.

SSI – Supplemental Security Income (Title XVI Benefits)
Government welfare program that provides cash assistance and healthcare coverage to people with low income and limited assets who are at least 65 years old, disabled, or blind.

SVP – Specific Vocational Preparation
The amount of time that it takes a person to learn a specific job.

Social Security Disability Vernacular (cont.)

Commonly Used Terms

Application for Benefits – To receive Social Security benefits (SSDI), Supplemental Security Income (SSI) payments, or Medicare, you must complete, sign, and apply to SSA. Applications can be submitted at one of the local field offices, over the telephone, or online at www.ssa.gov.

Benefits – Social Security pays five types of benefits: 1) Retirement, 2) Disability, 3) Family (dependents), 4) Survivors, and 5) Medicare. The retirement, family (dependents), survivor, and disability programs pay monthly cash benefits; Medicare provides medical coverage.

Credits – As you work and pay Social Security taxes, you earn credits that count toward your eligibility for future Social Security benefits. You can earn a maximum of four credits each year. Most people need 40 credits to qualify for benefits.

Early Retirement Age – 62 years old.

Insured Status – You have insured status if you worked and earned enough Social Security credits to be eligible for retirement or disability benefits or to enable your dependents to be eligible for benefits due to your retirement, disability, or death. **Retroactive Benefits (Back Pay)** – Monthly benefits that you may be entitled to receive before the month you apply, if you meet the requirements.

Survivors Benefits – If you should die, survivor benefits based on your record are paid to your widow/widower age 60 or older, 50 or older if disabled, or any age if caring for a child under age 16 or disabled before age 22; children, if they are unmarried and under age 18, under 19 but still in school, or 18 or older but disabled before age 22; and parents, if you provided at least one-half of their support. An ex-spouse could also be eligible for a widow/widower's benefit on your record. A special one-time lump sum payment of $255 may be made to your spouse or minor children.

Social Security Disability Vernacular (cont.)

Residual Functional Capacity (RFC) Levels:

- **Sedentary work** – This means you can lift no more than ten pounds at a time, and you only occasionally lift or carry things like files or small tools. A sedentary job mostly involves sitting, but you must be able to walk and stand occasionally.
- **Light work** – This means you can lift up to 20 pounds occasionally, and you frequently lift or carry up to 10 pounds. Light work requires frequent walking and standing and the ability to push and pull with your arms or legs. If you can do light work, you can do sedentary work.
- **Medium work** – This means you can lift up to 50 pounds at a time, and you frequently lift or carry up to 25 pounds. If you can do medium work, you can also do light and sedentary work.
- **Heavy work** – This means you can lift up to 100 pounds at a time, and you frequently lift or carry up to 50 pounds. If you can do heavy work, you can do medium, light, or sedentary work.
- **Very heavy work** – This means you can lift objects that weigh more than 100 pounds, and you frequently lift or carry 50 pounds or more. If you can do very heavy work, you can do all other levels as well.

Skill Level: SSA defines a skill as knowledge of a task that requires judgment and that is attained through job performance. In simpler terms, skills are the things you learned on your job, which were needed to make informed decisions and to accomplish tasks required to complete your work.

- **Unskilled Work** – Unskilled work requires little or no judgment to perform simple tasks and can usually be learned in less than a month. Doing unskilled work does not help a person gain work skills. Unskilled work often requires strength, but not always.
- **Semi-skilled Work** – Semi-skilled work requires some skills but doesn't include complex job functions. Semi-skilled work usually requires the ability to remain alert and pay attention to details in order to protect against risks. A job that requires quick movements of the hands and feet (in other words, coordination and dexterity) to perform a repetitive task can be classified as semi-skilled. A person usually needs between three and six months to learn a semi-skilled job.
- **Skilled Work** – Skilled work requires specific qualifications, the use of judgment, and knowing how to perform mechanical or manual tasks to create a product or material or to provide a service. Skilled work may also include reading specifications, measuring, estimating, and making calculations. Skilled work can include jobs that require a person to work closely with others or to know figures, facts, or ideas that require complex, abstract, or critical thinking. It takes at least six months and often many years to train for and learn a skilled job.

Preliminary Test

Do I qualify for Social Security Disability Insurance (SSDI)?

Please answer the following questions:

1) Have you worked approximately 5 of the past 10 years?

    YES   or   NO

2) Are you unable to work due to a serious physical or mental medical condition?

    YES   or   NO

3) Is your medical condition expected to last at least 12 months or result in death?

    YES   or   NO

4) Are you 18 or older?

    YES   or   NO

Note: You must be able to answer "YES" to each of these questions to continue filing electronically.

Please answer these follow-up questions:

A. Are you currently receiving SSDI benefits?

    YES   or   NO

B. Have you been denied benefits within the past 60 days?

    YES   or   NO

Note: You must be able to answer "NO" to each question to continue filing electronically.

Initial Application Online Filing Checklist

What you'll need to file electronically:

1) A computer or mobile device with Internet access

2) A *my* Social Security account (strongly recommended)

3) Information about your background, marital history, and children

4) Information about your employment history

5) Information about your education history and training

6) Information about your medical condition(s)

7) Information about your doctors, specialists, and healthcare providers

8) Your information for the bank account where you want your Social Security benefits deposited if you're approved

Creating a *my* Social Security Account

Skip this step if you already have an account.

To create a *my* Social Security account, go to https://www.ssa.gov/myaccount/

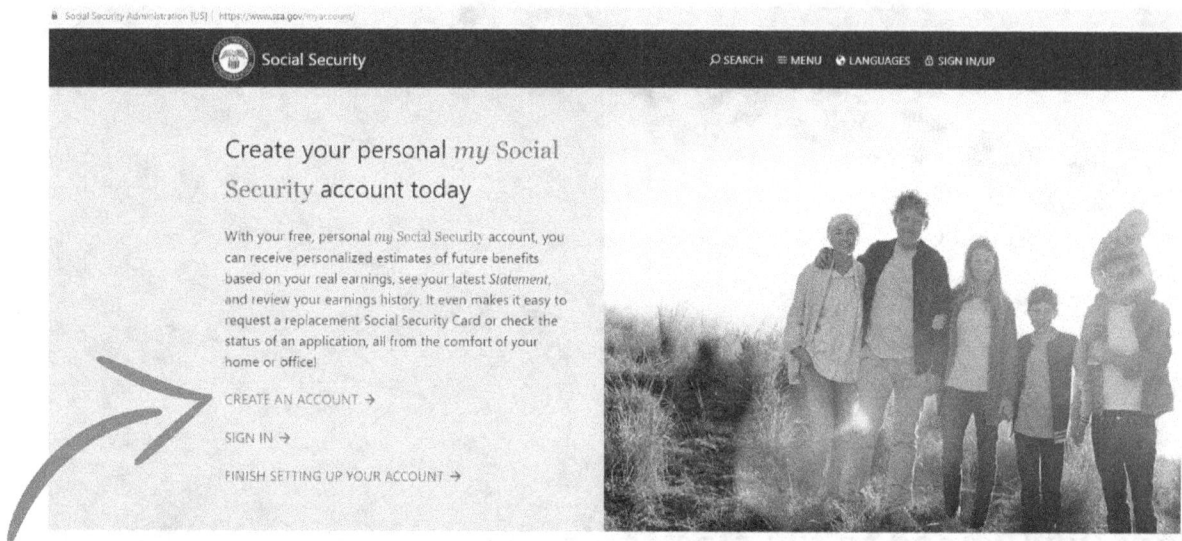

Click the **"CREATE AN ACCOUNT"** hyperlink.

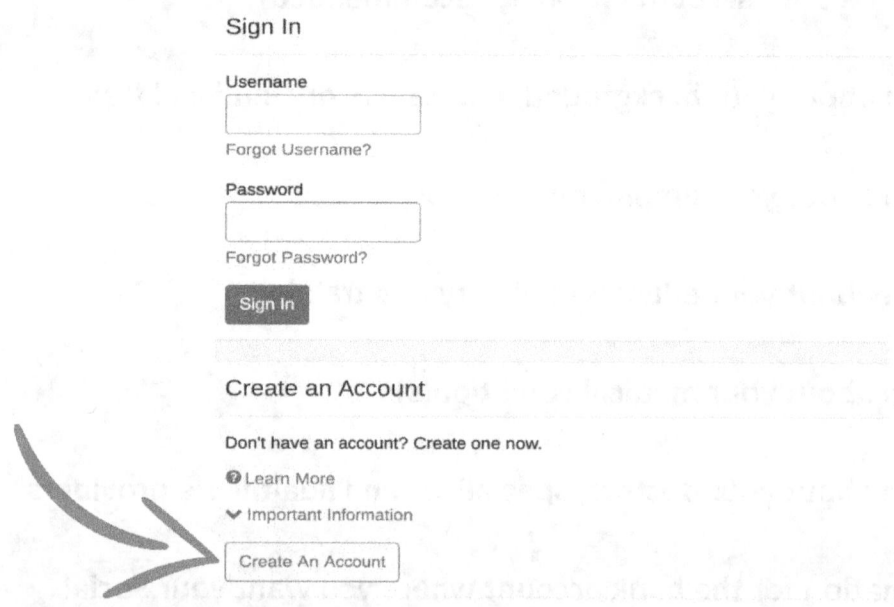

Then click the **"Create An Account"** button.

You'll then be prompted to enter your information.

If you so desire, you can add an extra layer of security. I highly recommend taking this precaution if you share your living space with other people.

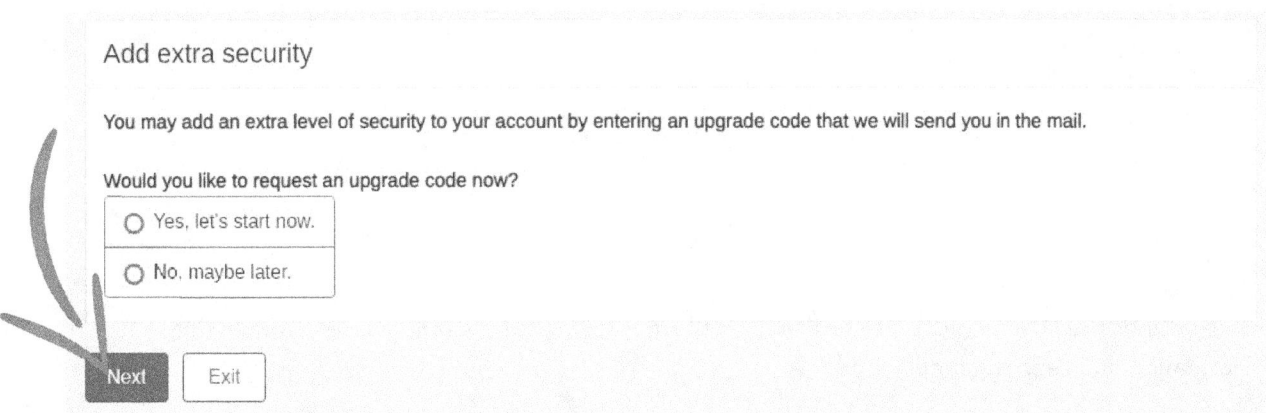

Click the **"Next"** button to continue.

You'll then be asked a series of multiple-choice questions to confirm your identity.

Questions may include:

- Which financial institution holds your mortgage?
- Which bank is the lender on a car loan?
- What are the last 4 digits of your mobile phone (current or past)?
- Have you ever lived on one of the following streets?

 Note: Be aware that in order to continue, you must respond correctly to every question. If you answer a question incorrectly, you'll likely receive an error notice informing you that your account has been suspended for 24 hours.

I know how difficult it may be to remember different financial accounts, telephone numbers, and other data from long ago. I initially had trouble with this myself. To unlock your account, please call (800) 772-1213 and say "help desk" when prompted.

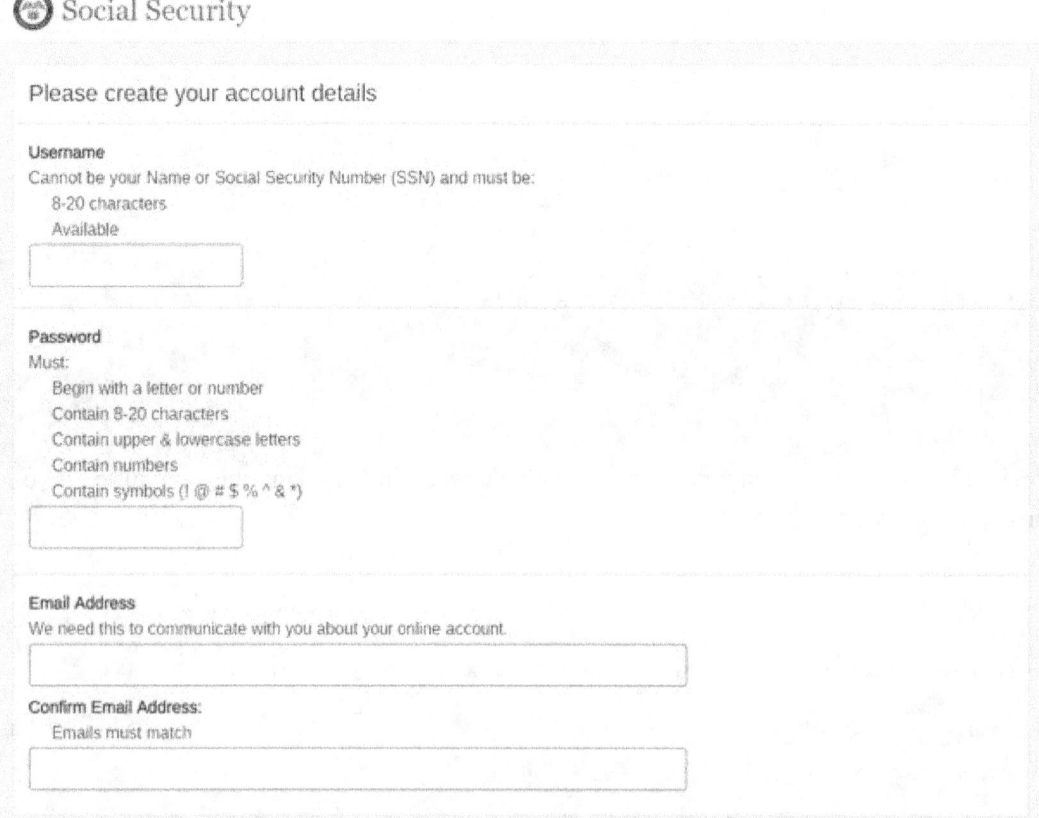

Enter your desired username, password, and email address. Make sure that you write down this information and keep it someplace handy.

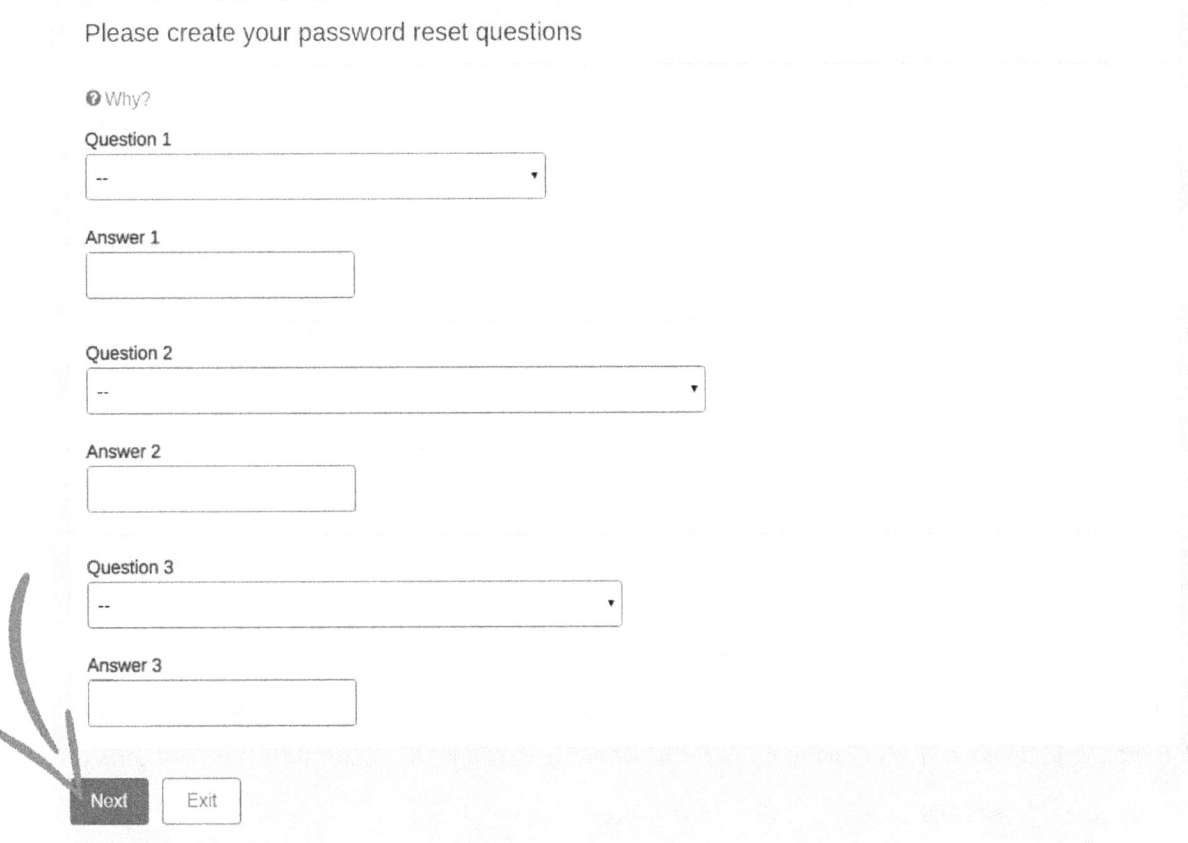

In case you forget your login information, you'll be prompted to choose your own questions to reset your password.

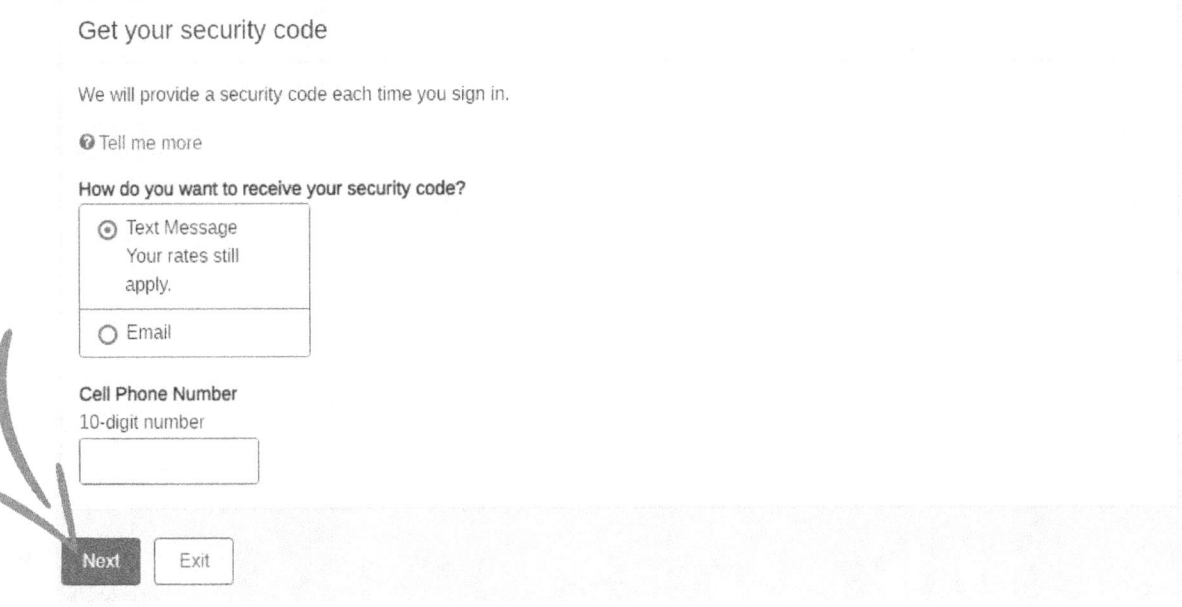

If you so desire, you can also opt to have a security code texted to your mobile phone for extra security whenever you sign in.

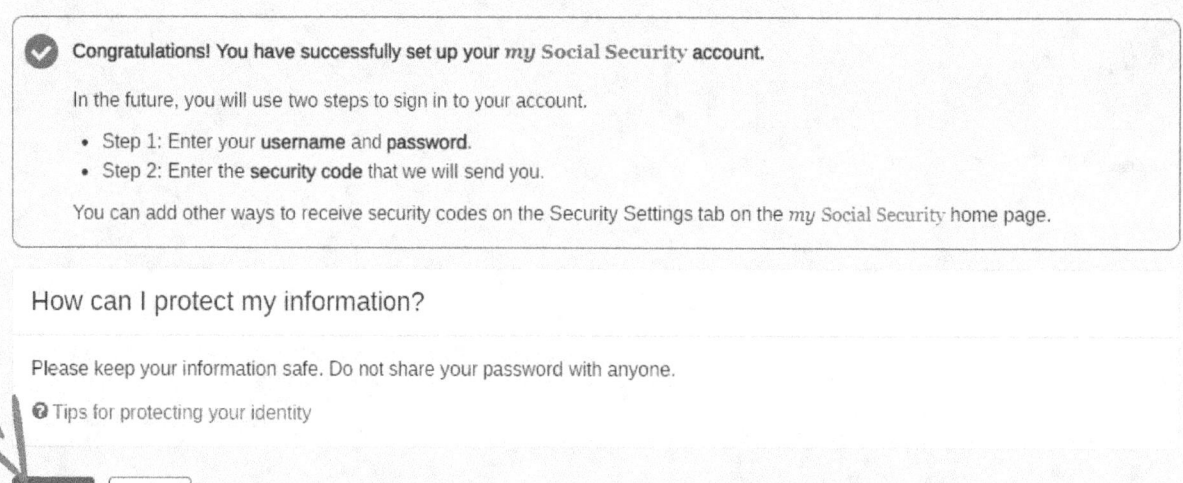

Voilà! You've created a *my* Social Security account!

Now you'll have an easier time reviewing your earnings history and managing your benefits. You'll also be able to get an estimate of how much your monthly benefits would be if you became disabled today.

You're ready to apply for SSDI now.

Now Let's Begin!

Getting Started:

First, go to https://www.ssa.gov/benefits/disability/

Then click the "**Apply for Disability**" button, as shown below.

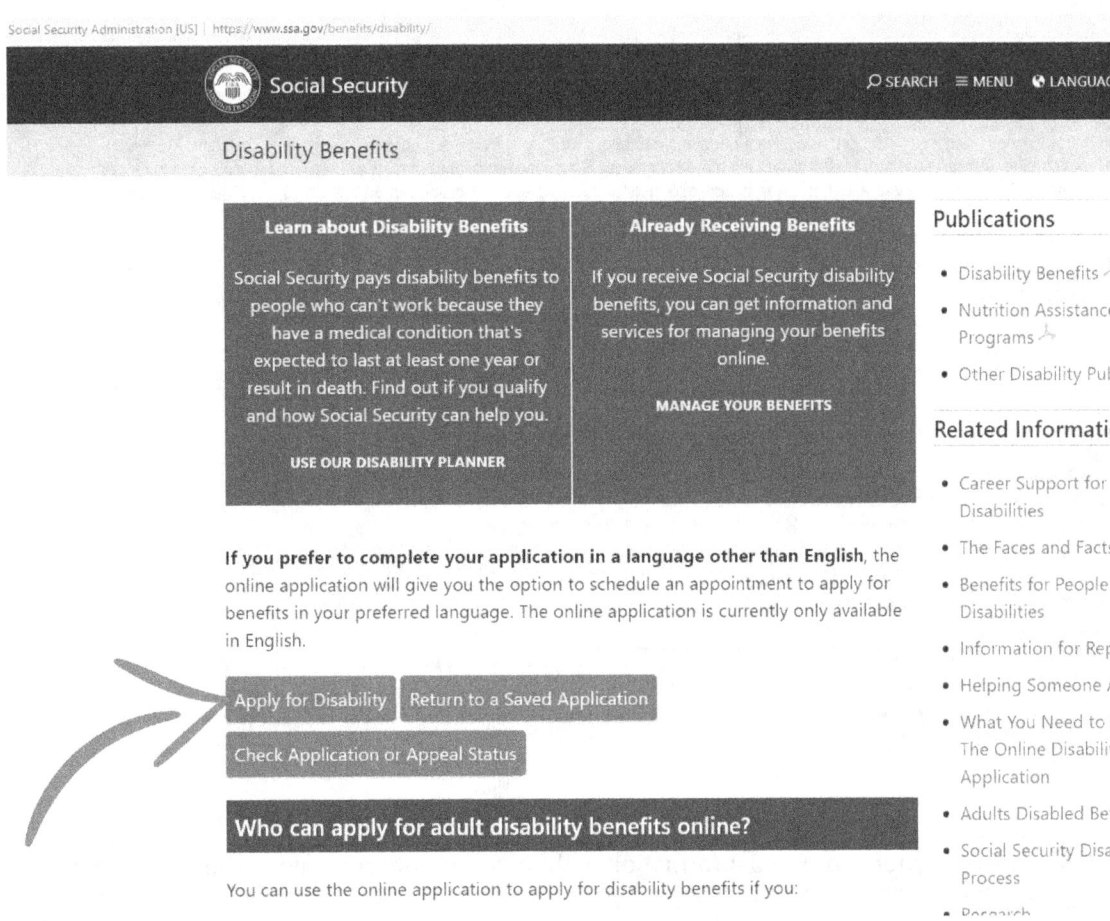

Review the Terms of Service:

Click the "**I understand...**" check box, then click the "**Next**" button to begin, as shown below.

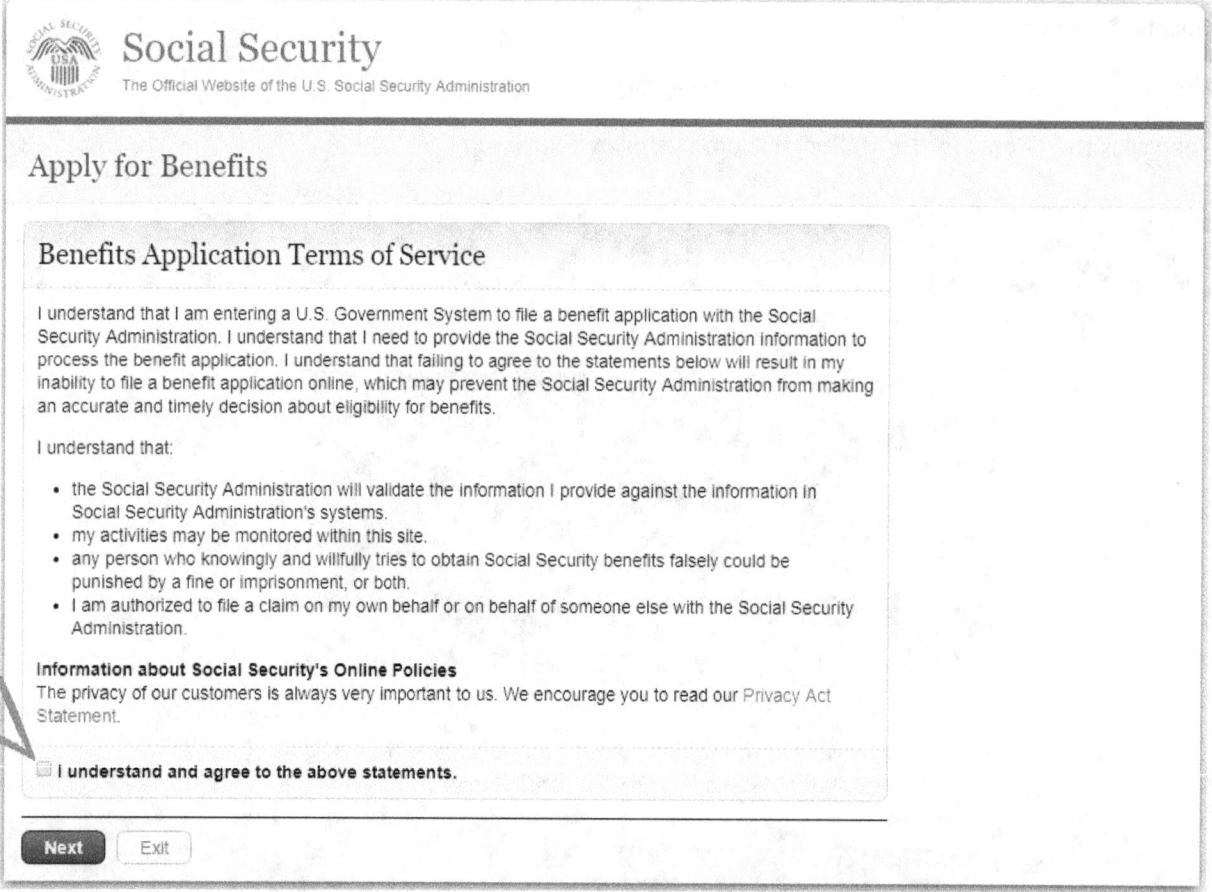

Key Points:

- SSA will compare your submitted information with the information on file, so be candid in your responses.
- SSA will monitor and review state records (e.g., earnings, criminal record, etc.).
- If you intend to defraud SSA to collect benefits, you could face criminal punishment.
- You should file only for yourself or on behalf of someone who has given you permission to file.

On this page, you'll choose whether you're applying for yourself or for someone else.

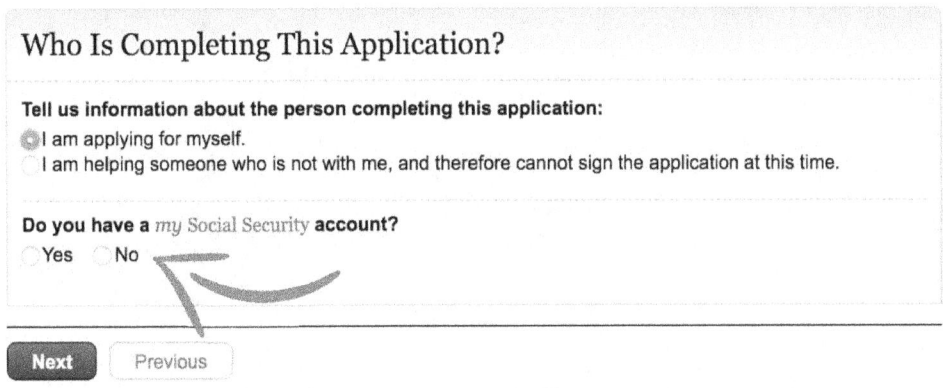

Don't forget to state whether you have a *my* Social Security account.

Click "**Yes**" to log into your *my* Social Security account on the next screen.

If you opted not to create a *my* Social Security account, select "**No**."

Then confirm that you have an address in the U.S.

Terms of Service

- I am using *my* Social Security account services with the account that I created myself using my own personal information and identity. I am not using a *my* Social Security account created by another person or created using another person's information or identity, even if I have that person's written permission.
- I will never share the use of *my* Social Security account with anyone else under any circumstances. I will never use another person's *my* Social Security account.
- I understand that *my* Social Security account contains U.S. Government information.
- I consent to the monitoring and recording of my use of *my* Social Security services, including any electronic communications (such as click-to-chat or messaging).
- I understand that it is a federal crime to:
    - Give false or misleading statements to obtain information in Social Security records; or
    - Deceive the Social Security Administration about an individual's identity.
- I understand that unauthorized use of *my* Social Security services is a misrepresentation of my identity to the federal government and could subject me to criminal or civil penalties, or both.
- I understand that the Social Security Administration may stop me from using *my* Social Security services online if it finds or suspects misuse.
- I accept that the responsibility to properly protect any information provided to me by the Social Security Administration is mine and that I am the responsible party should any information on or from my computer or other device be improperly disclosed.
- I agree that the Social Security Administration is not responsible for the improper disclosure of any information that the Social Security Adminstration has provided to me, whether due to my negligence or the wrongful acts of others.

The Social Security Administration is Going "Green"

With your *my* Social Security account, you can immediately view, download, or print your Social Security Statement. Your online *Statement* contains the most up-to-date information in our records about your earnings and benefit.

Remember, now that you have a *my* Social Security account, you will no longer receive a paper *Statement* in the mail. If you need a *Statement* by mail, please follow these instructions.

☑ I agree to the Terms of Service.

[Next] [Exit]

Once you click the "**Next**" button, you'll be able to view your Social Security statement and earnings history.

If you didn't create a *my* Social Security account, the page below is the first page of the application.

Input your full legal name, Social Security number, DOB, and gender.

Then state whether or not you're blind.

Apply for Benefits

⚠ **You did not create or sign into your** *my* Social Security **account.**
Please provide the information below so we can determine if you may continue with the application.

Information About Applicant

Your Name:
Please provide the name as it appears on the most recent Social Security card.

[First] [Middle] [Last] [-- ▼ Suffix]

Social Security Number (SSN):
[   ]

Date of Birth:
[-- ▼ Month] [Day] [Year]

Gender:
○ Male ○ Female

Are you blind or do you have low vision even with glasses or contacts?
○ Yes ○ No

During the last 14 months, have you been unable to work because of illnesses, injuries or conditions that have lasted or are expected to last at least 12 months or can be expected to result in death? ❓ More Info
○ Yes ○ No

[**Next**] [Exit]

 Warning: You must be able to answer "**Yes**" on the last question to continue.

Click the "**Next**" button to continue.

Once you click the "**Yes**" button, you'll see the following questions:

> **During the last 14 months, have you been unable to work because of illnesses, injuries or conditions that have lasted or are expected to last at least 12 months or can be expected to result in death?** More Info
>
> ◉ Yes ○ No
>
> **What date did you become unable to work?**
>
> -- ▼   -- ▼   -- ▼
> Month Day   Year
>
> **Have you previously been denied for Social Security benefits or Supplemental Security Income (SSI) in the last 60 days?**
>
> ○ Yes ○ No
>
> **Have you been diagnosed with any specific condition that is expected to end in death?**
>
> ○ Yes ○ No
>
> [Next] [Exit]

Input the date that you last worked or the date that you feel you became unable to work.

Note: The date must be in the past. If you're currently working but intend to stop working soon, you must wait until you stop working before applying for benefits.

State whether you've been previously denied SSDI or SSI benefits **in the last 60 days**.

Note: Must be able to answer "**No**" to continue. If you answer "**Yes**," you'll need to file an appeal instead or wait 60 days from the date of denial to apply again.

State whether you've been diagnosed with any specific condition that is expected to end in death.

Note: This is for serious medical conditions only, where a prognosis given by your doctor indicates that you may have less than twelve months to live (e.g., cancer).

If you choose "**Yes**," your claim will be expedited.

Click the "**Next**" button to continue.

You may briefly see this screen:

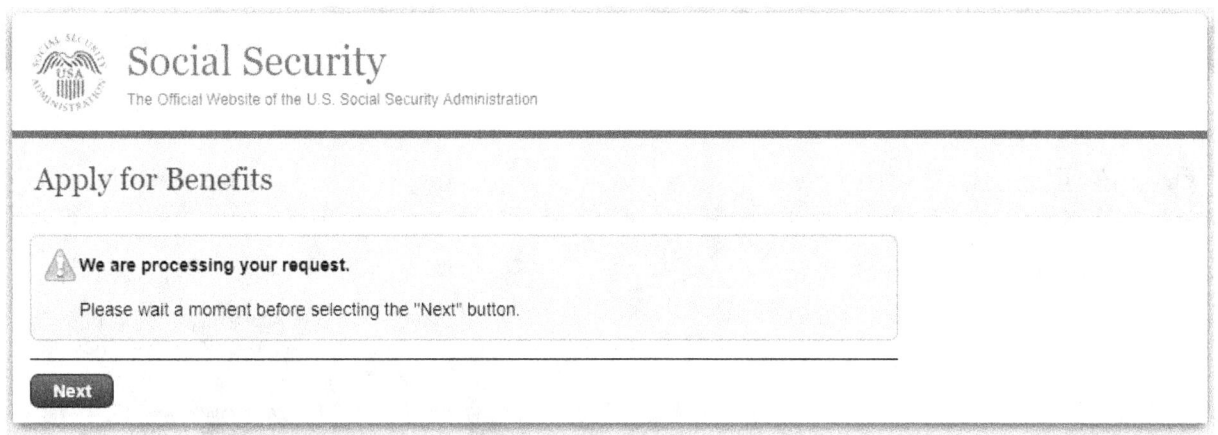

Note: This indicates that you're on Step 1 of 4 of the application.

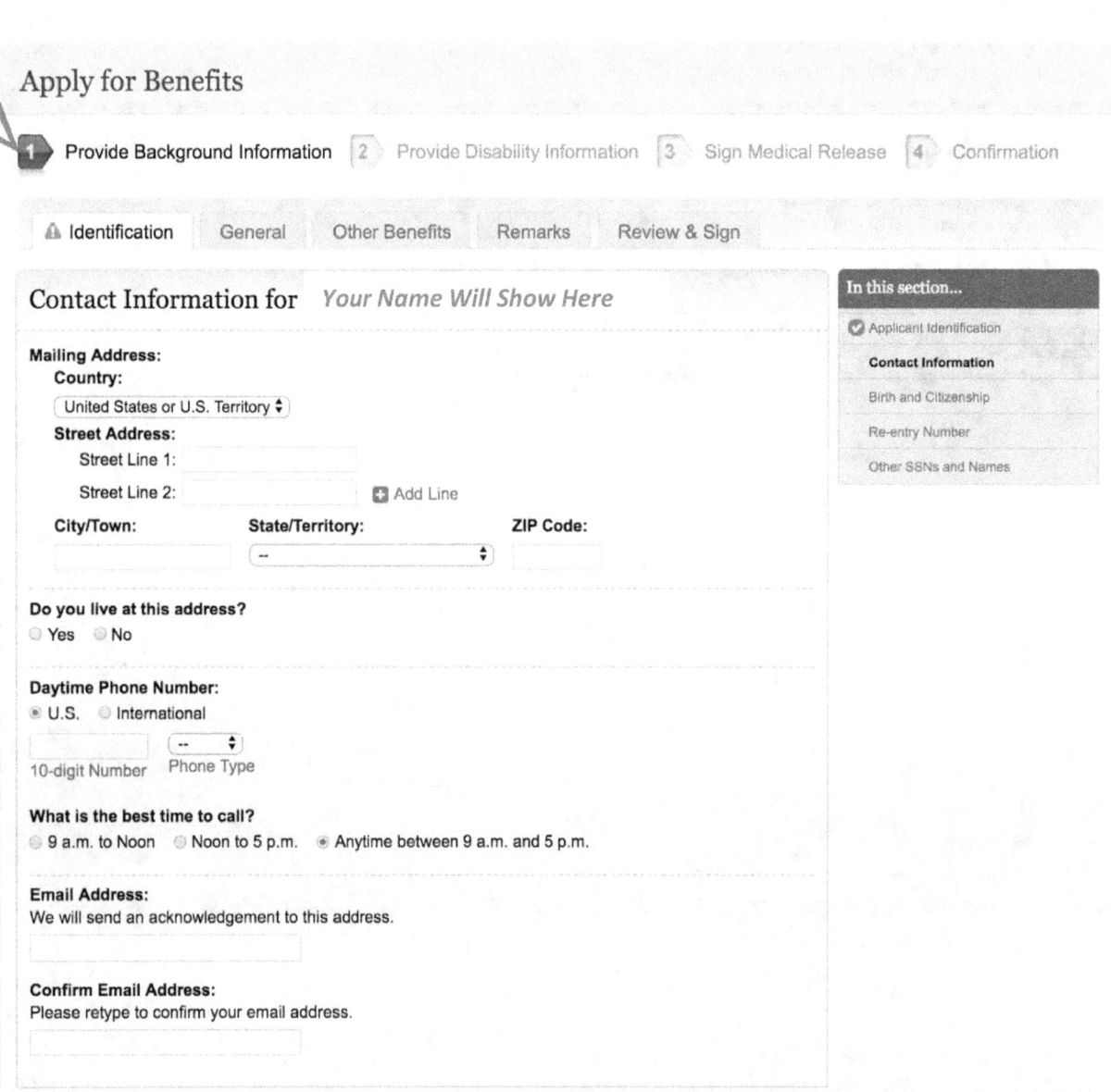

Input your contact information and email address.

You'll receive communications concerning your disability application at this email address, so be sure to check it regularly.

Email Address:
We will send an acknowledgement to this address.

Confirm Email Address:
Please retype to confirm your email address.

Ability to Communicate in English

Can you speak and understand English?
◉ Yes ○ No

Can you read and understand English?
◉ Yes ○ No

Can you write more than your name in English?
◉ Yes ○ No

Language Preferences for *Your Name Will Show Here*

Language preferred for speaking:
[English ▼]

Language preferred for reading:
[English ▼]

[**Next**] [Previous]

Select your language preference, both for speaking and for reading.

Note: If English is NOT your first language and you have difficulty speaking or reading English, I recommend that you select the language you are most comfortable speaking and reading to ensure that you understand all the questions and are able to provide accurate responses.

Click the "**Next**" button to continue.

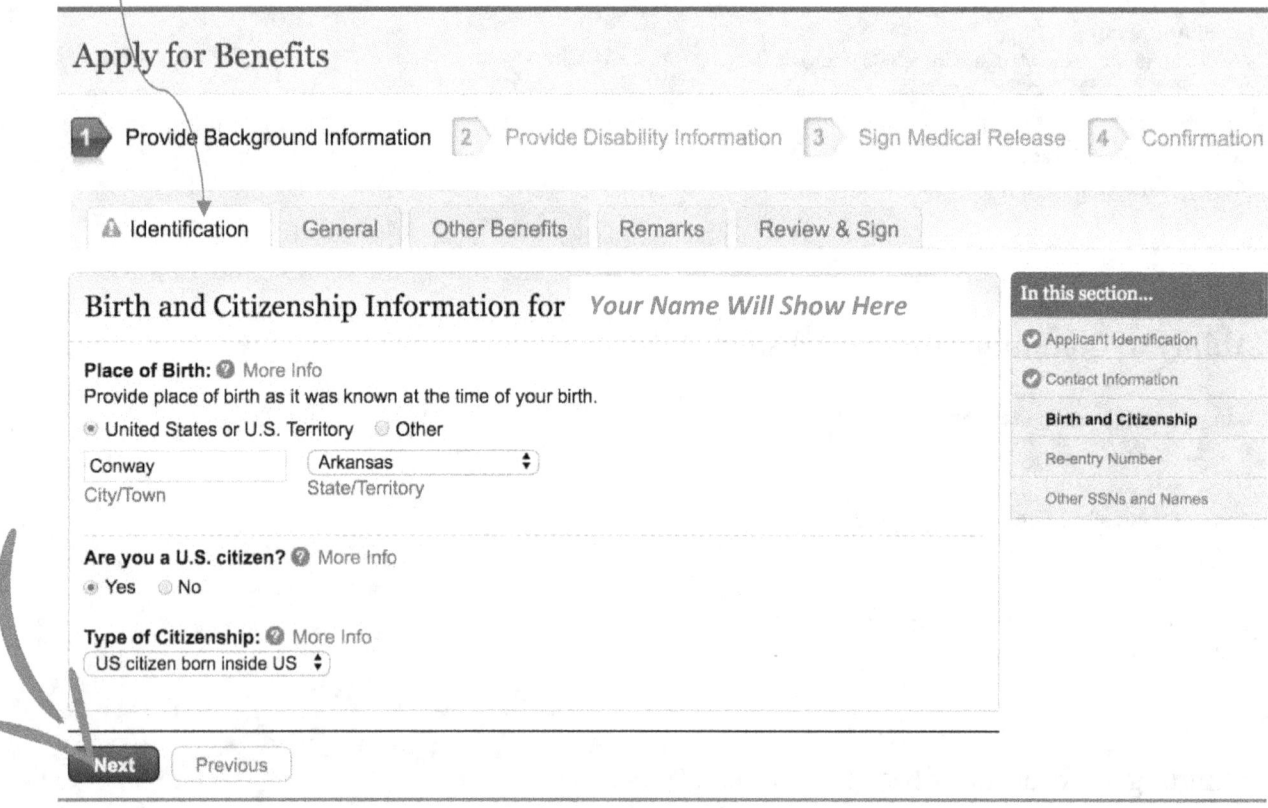

Input your place of birth and your citizenship information.

Click the "**Next**" button to continue.

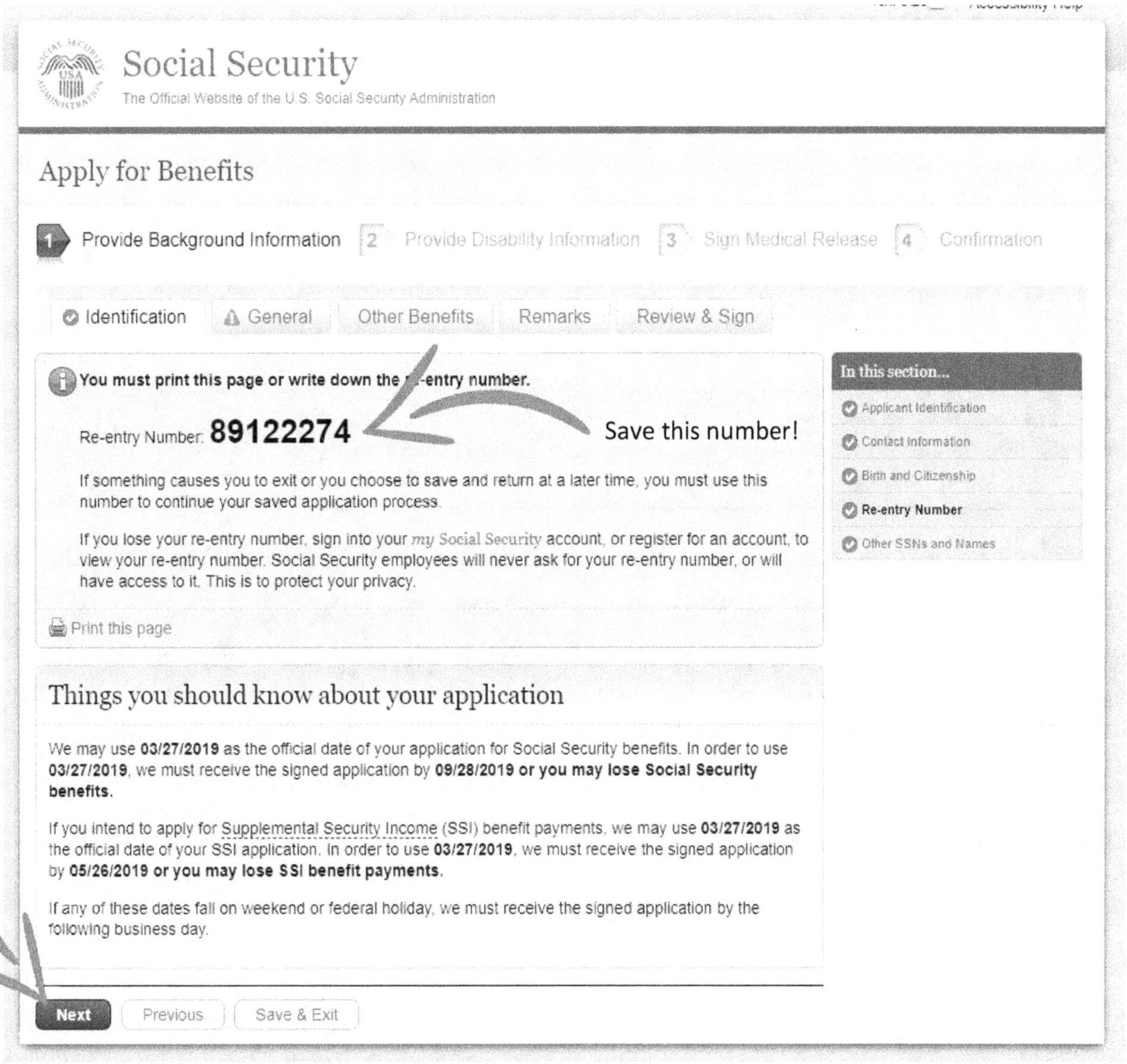

This page will give you a "Re-entry Number."

Please be sure to keep this number somewhere handy.

Tip: Send yourself an email with **"RE-ENTRY NUMBER"** in the subject line and your unique number in the body. This way you can always find it by simply searching your email inbox.

At this point of your application, SSA may use today's date as the official date of your application for Social Security benefits. You must complete the application within 6 months from today to preserve this date (or 2 months from today for SSI benefits).

Click the "**Next**" button to continue.

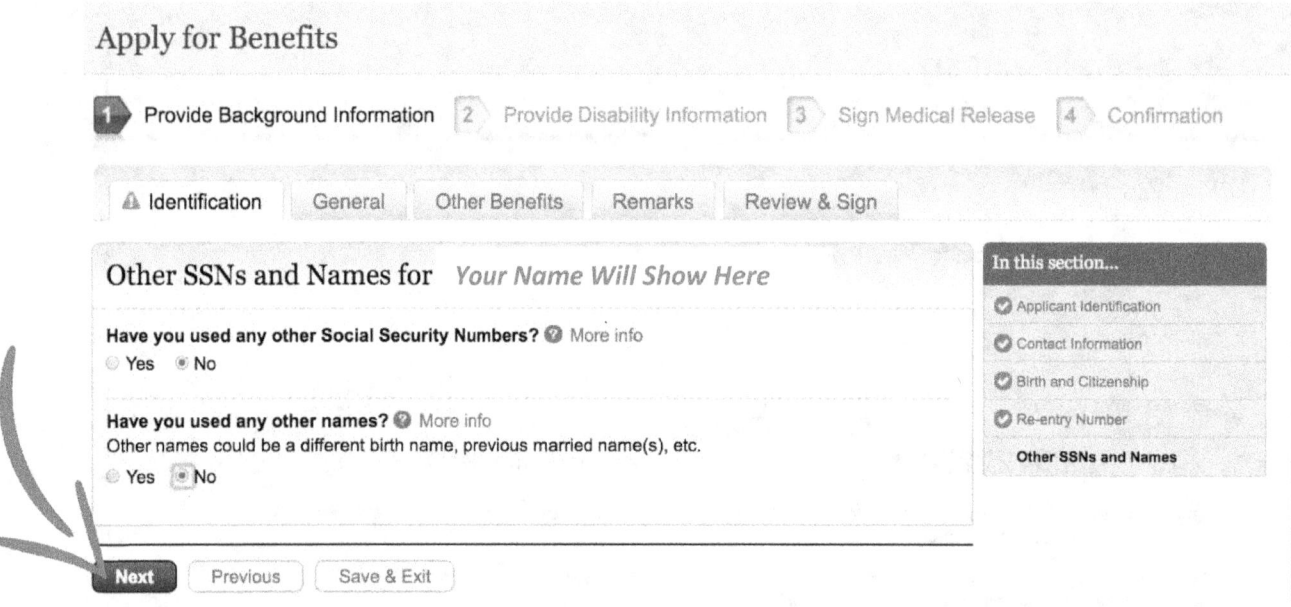

State whether you've used any other Social Security numbers.

State whether you've used any other name(s). This is important because if you've ever used any other name(s) in the past, you may have very important medical records under your other name(s), which may be helpful in the evaluation of your claim for disability.

Click the "**Next**" button to continue.

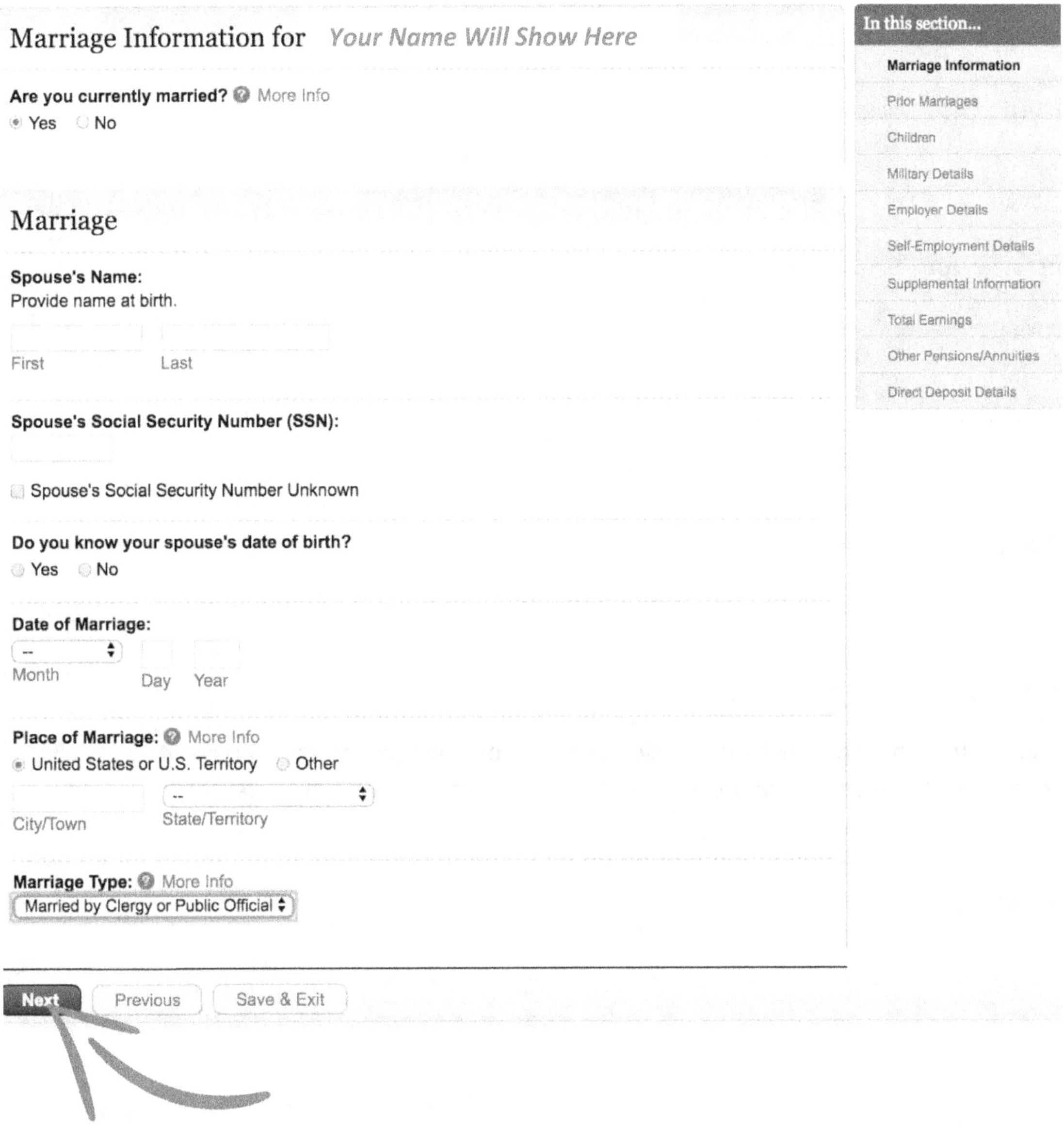

If you're not married, then select "**No**" to continue. If you are married, then input information about your spouse and your marriage.

Click the "**Next**" button to continue.

Note: If you're not sure about your answers to any of these questions, you'll have an opportunity later in the application process to make comments concerning previous questions. For example, if you don't recall the exact date or place of your marriage, you can input your best guess on this screen, and later you can indicate that you're uncertain of your response.

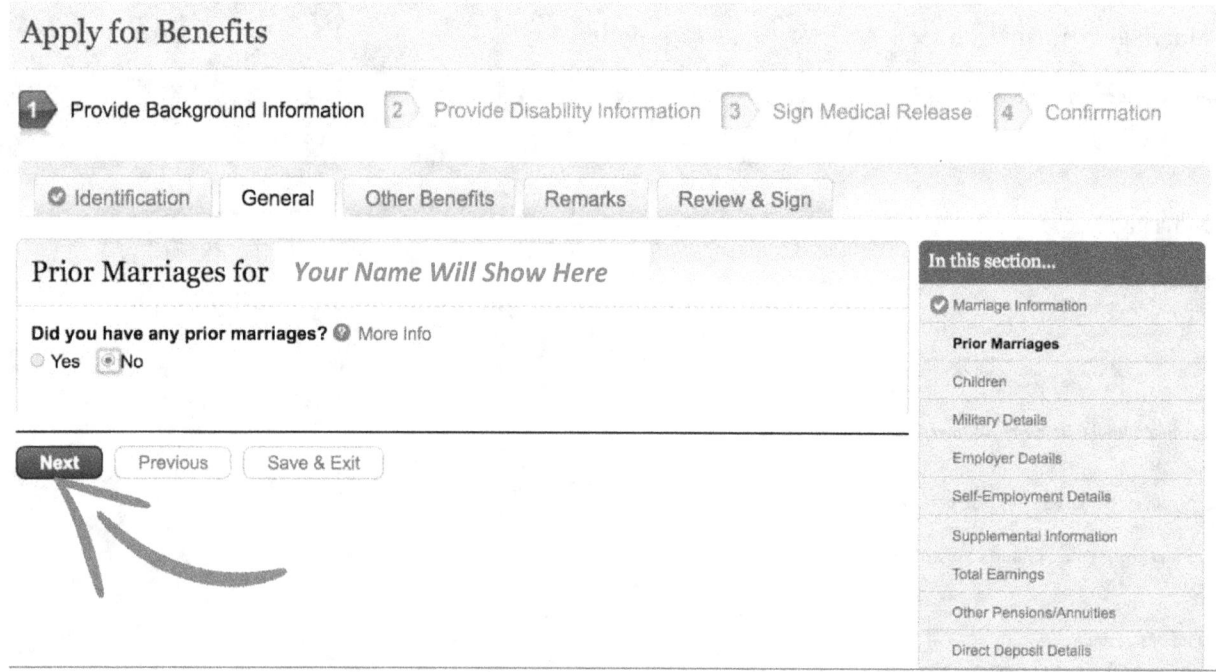

Indicate whether you've had any prior marriages.

If your answer is "**Yes**," input as much information as possible about your former spouse. If you can't remember exact dates, you can use approximate dates for now and correct the dates later.

Click the "**Next**" button to continue.

Indicate whether you have any children. If your answer is "**Yes**," then you'll need to enter information about each of your children. It's best to start with the oldest child first.

Children for *Your Name Will Show Here*

These questions also apply to children born out of wedlock, adopted children, and step-children. In certain cases, grandchildren and step-grandchildren who live with you may qualify for benefits. **Note:** If a child reached the age limit within the last twelve months, please answer "Yes."

Do you have any children?
◉ Yes   ○ No

Did any of your children become disabled prior to the age of 22?
○ Yes   ◉ No

Are any of your children unmarried and under age 18?
◉ Yes   ○ No

Are any of your children unmarried, aged 18 to 19, and still attending elementary or secondary school (below college level) full time?
○ Yes   ◉ No

Names of children for which you answered "Yes" above

Child's Name 1:

| J | Foster |
| First | Last |

Child's Name 10:

| | |
| First | Last |

Do you have more than 10 children in the categories above?
○ Yes   ◉ No

[Next] [Previous] [Save & Exit]

Select "**Yes**" if any of your children became disabled prior to the age of 22.

Select "**Yes**" if any of your children are unmarried and under the age of 18.

Select "**Yes**" if any of your children are unmarried, aged 18-19, and still attending school full-time (not college).

Click the "**Next**" button to continue.

State whether you were in the U.S. military prior to 1968.

State whether you're receiving or eligible to receive military or civilian Federal agency benefits. If "**Yes**," select the type of benefit in the drop-down menu.

Input details of "**Military Service**" at the bottom.

Click the "**Next**" button to continue.

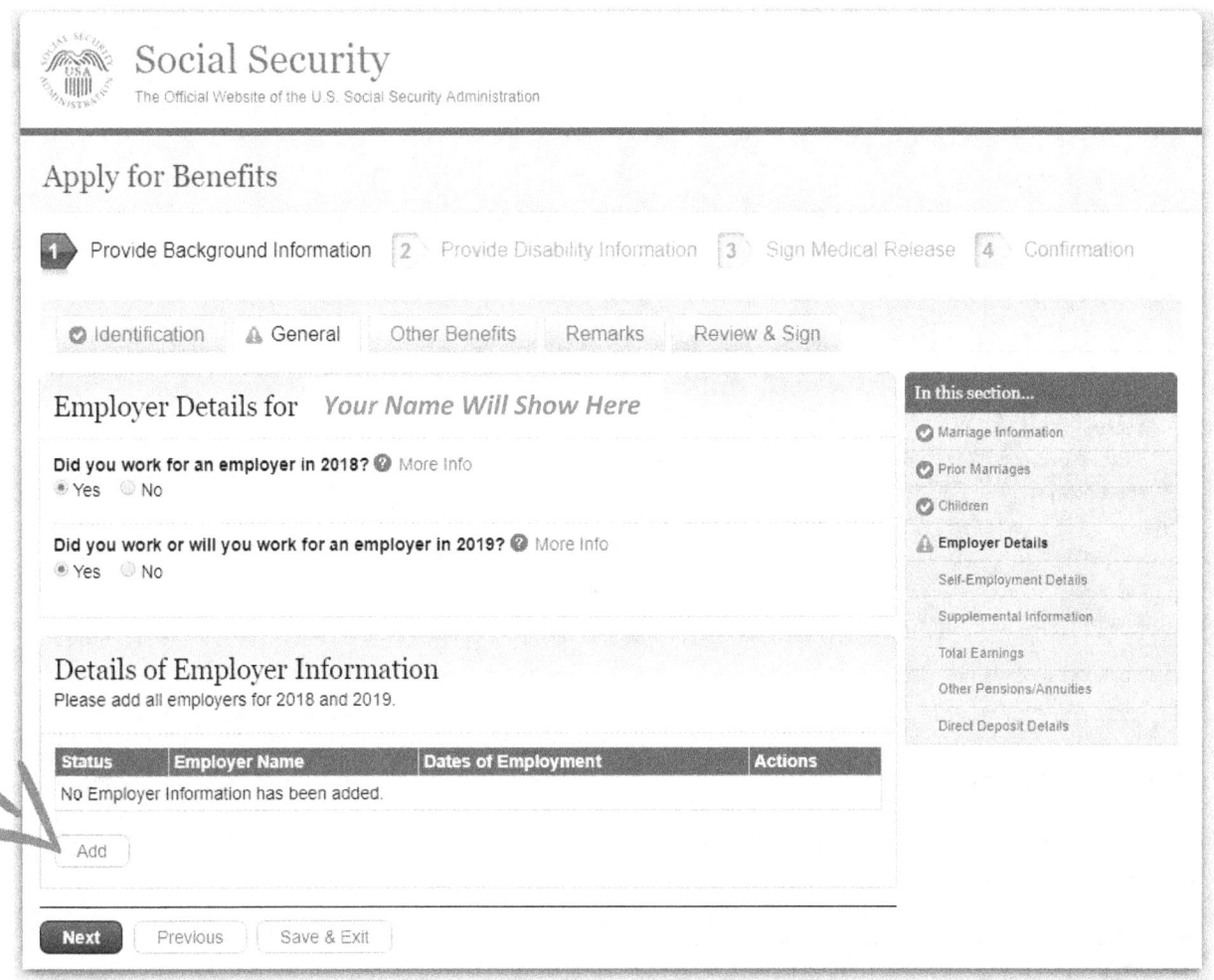

State whether you've worked for an employer at any point in the past 2 years.

If so, then click "**Add**" to add as many new employers as necessary.

Click the "**Next**" button to continue.

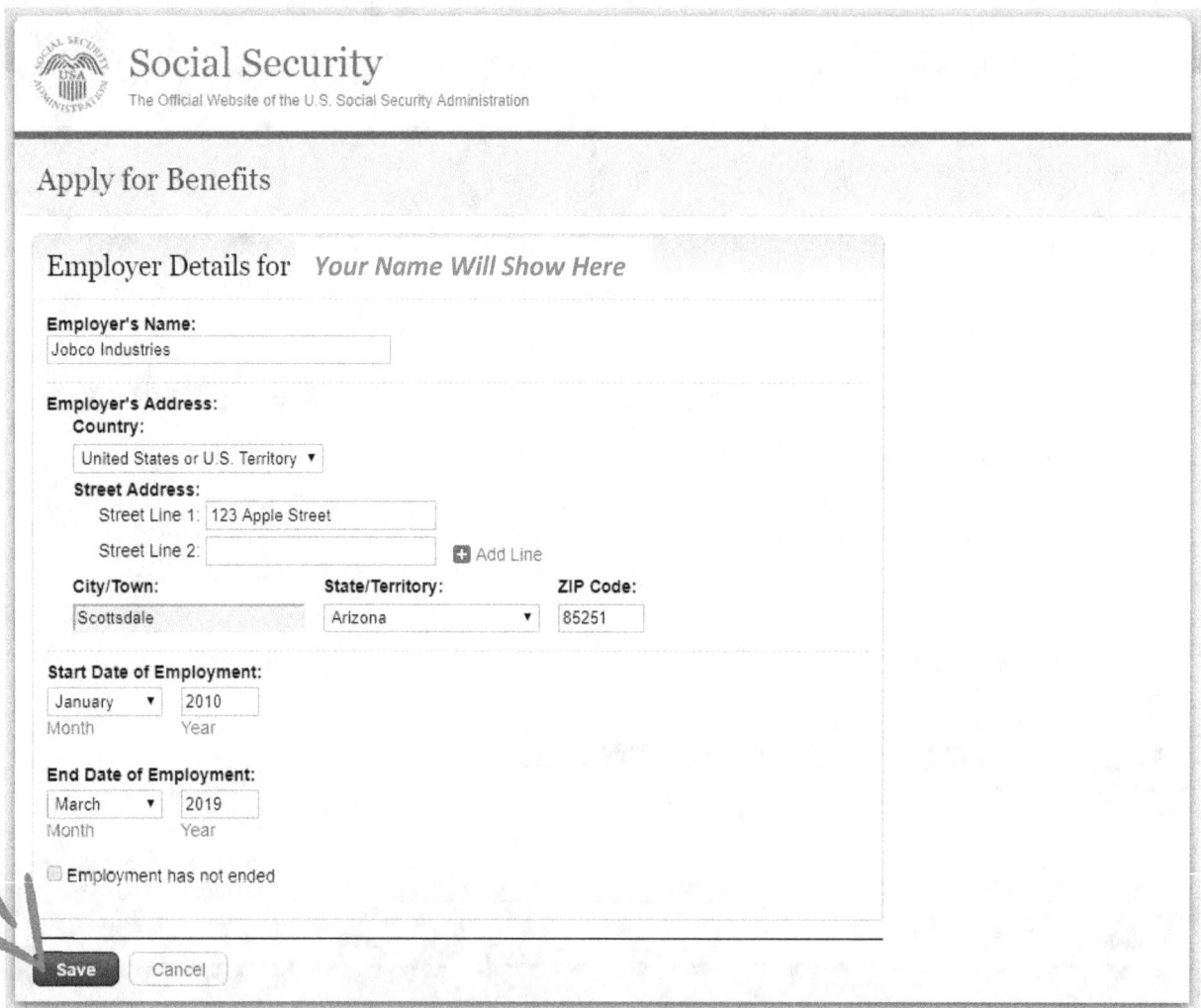

Fill out the above information for each employer at every job you've held for the past 2 years.

Click the "**Save**" button to save the information, then return to the "**Employer Details**" screen.

Click the "**Add**" button to add additional employers for 2018 and 2019.

Click the "**Next**" button to continue to the "Self-Employment Details" screen.

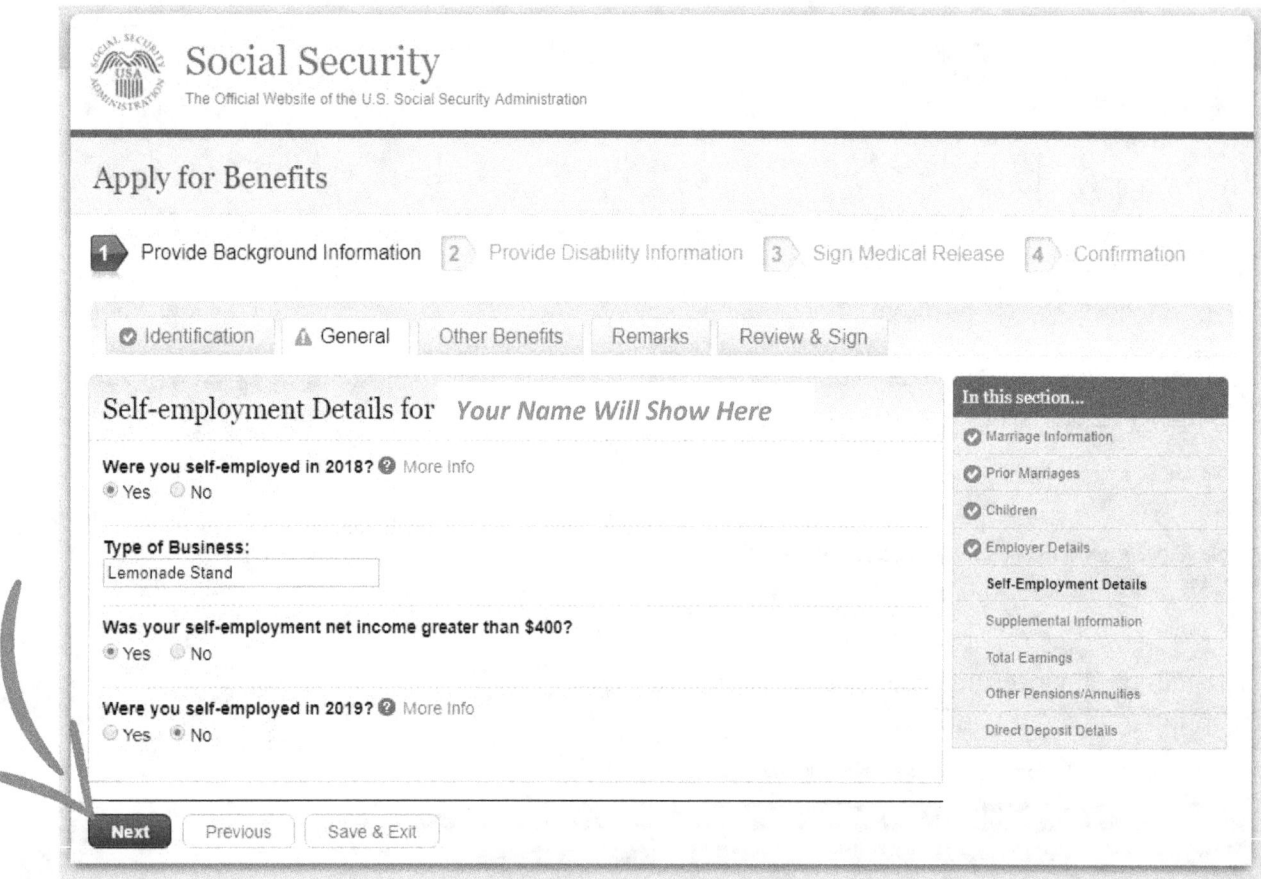

Here you'll answer questions about self-employment.

If you were self-employed in 2018, select "**Yes**" and input the type of business.

 Note: You should describe in general terms what type of business you owned.

Indicate whether your "net income" (gross income minus expenses) was greater than $400 for 2018.

Indicate whether you were self-employed in 2019.

Click the "**Next**" button to continue.

Next, answer the questions about whether you or your spouse worked outside of the United States.

Then state whether you agree with your earnings history, as shown on your Social Security Statement. If you don't know for certain, then you can mark "**Not sure**."

Note: If you created a *my* Social Security account, I strongly encourage you to review your earnings record before answering this question. If you disagree with something on your statement, you can indicate "**No**" and seek to correct your statement.

Click the "**Next**" button to continue.

Here you'll input your total earnings for 2018 and 2019 (if applicable). If you didn't work in the past 2 years, you won't see this screen.

Then you'll state whether you received any "Special Payments."

Note: Special payments may include bonuses; vacation pay or sick leave; severance pay; back pay; non-work pay; sales commissions; or delayed or deferred compensation reported on a W-2 form for one year of earnings in a previous year.

Click the "**Next**" button to continue.

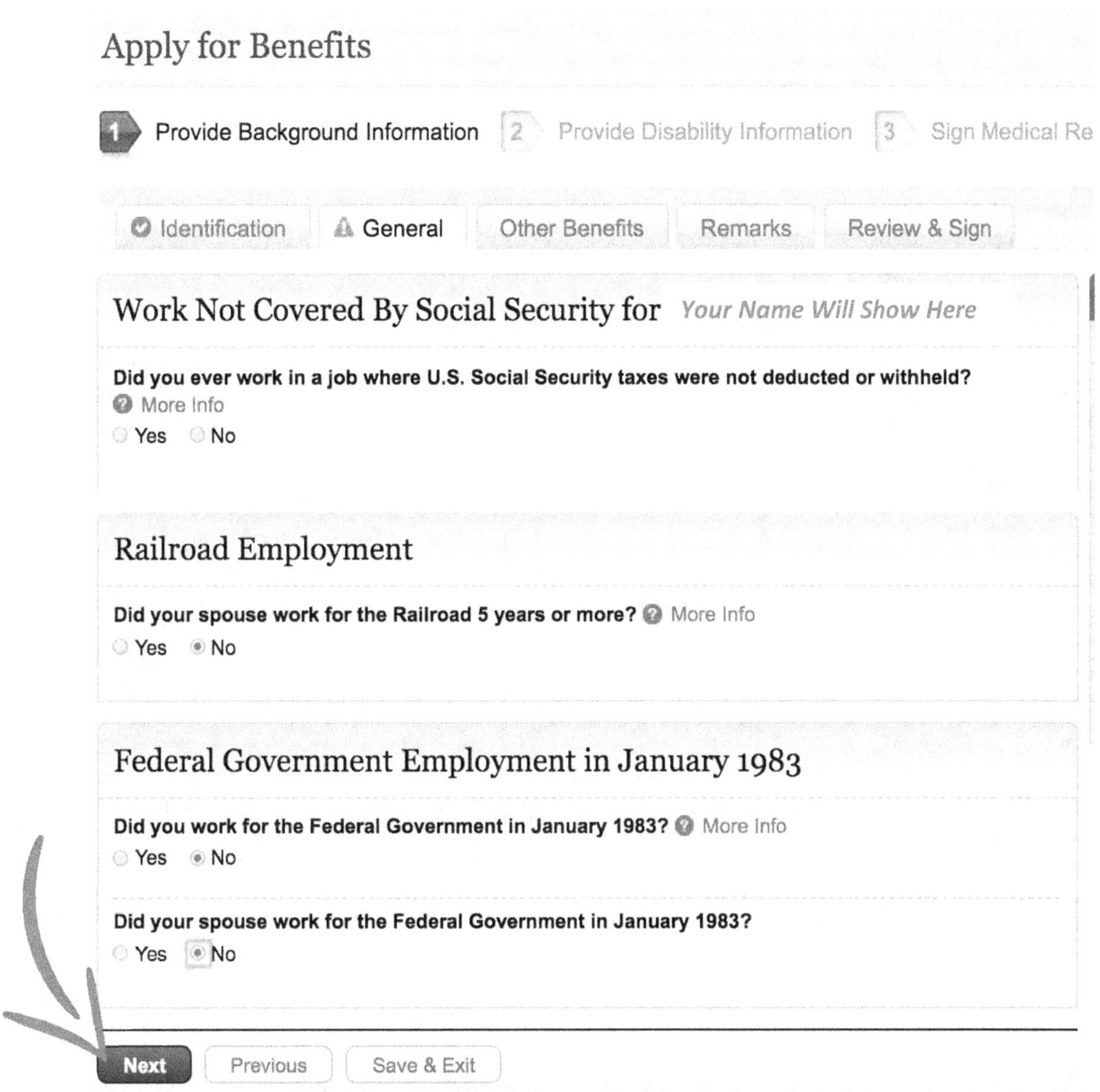

Apply for Benefits

1. Provide Background Information | 2. Provide Disability Information | 3. Sign Medical Re

Identification | **General** | Other Benefits | Remarks | Review & Sign

Work Not Covered By Social Security for *Your Name Will Show Here*

Did you ever work in a job where U.S. Social Security taxes were not deducted or withheld?
More Info
○ Yes ○ No

Railroad Employment

Did your spouse work for the Railroad 5 years or more? More Info
○ Yes ● No

Federal Government Employment in January 1983

Did you work for the Federal Government in January 1983? More Info
○ Yes ● No

Did your spouse work for the Federal Government in January 1983?
○ Yes ● No

[Next] [Previous] [Save & Exit]

Here you'll indicate whether you've ever worked a job where U.S. Social Security taxes weren't deducted or withheld.

Note: This includes work as a 1099-contractor, where taxes aren't deducted or withheld by the employer.

Then indicate if your spouse has worked for the Railroad for 5 years or more.

Lastly, indicate whether you worked for the Federal Government in January 1983.

Click the "**Next**" button to continue.

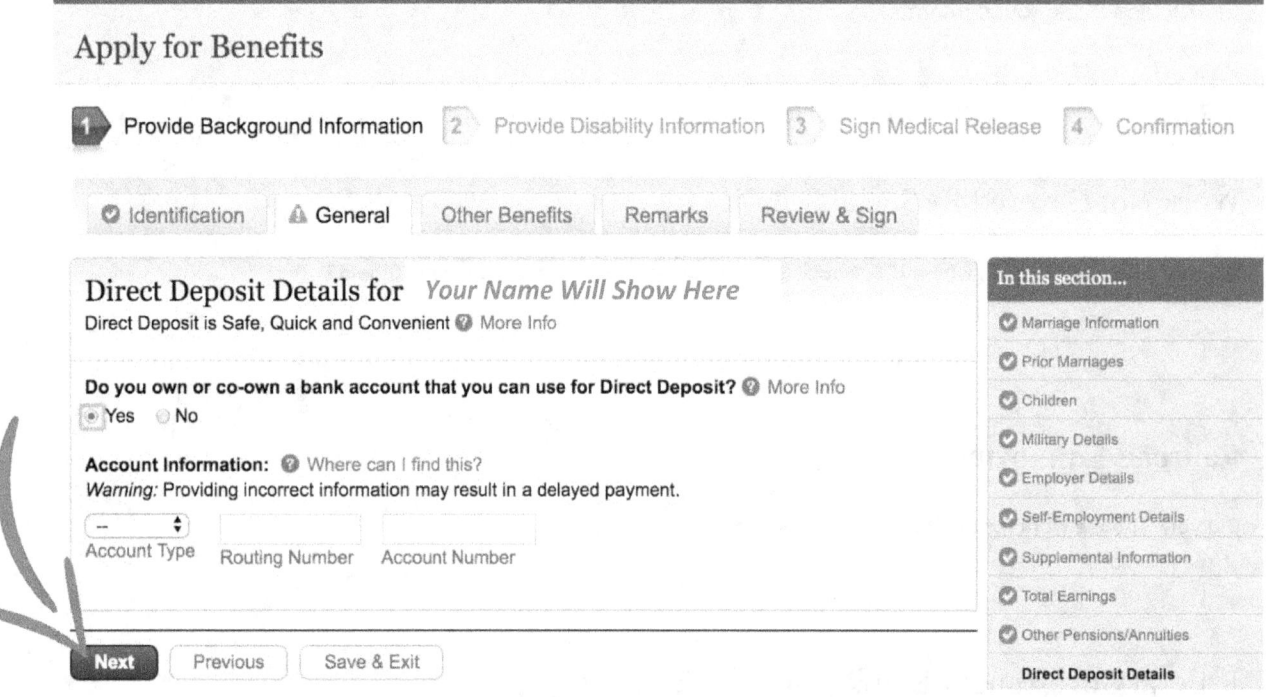

Here you'll input direct deposit details of your bank account. This is the account where Social Security will deposit monthly benefits.

You'll need to provide the following information:

- Account Type (checking or savings)
- Routing Number
- Account Number

If you select "**No**" because you don't have a bank account, you'll receive this message:

Click the "**Next**" button to continue.

Apply for Benefits

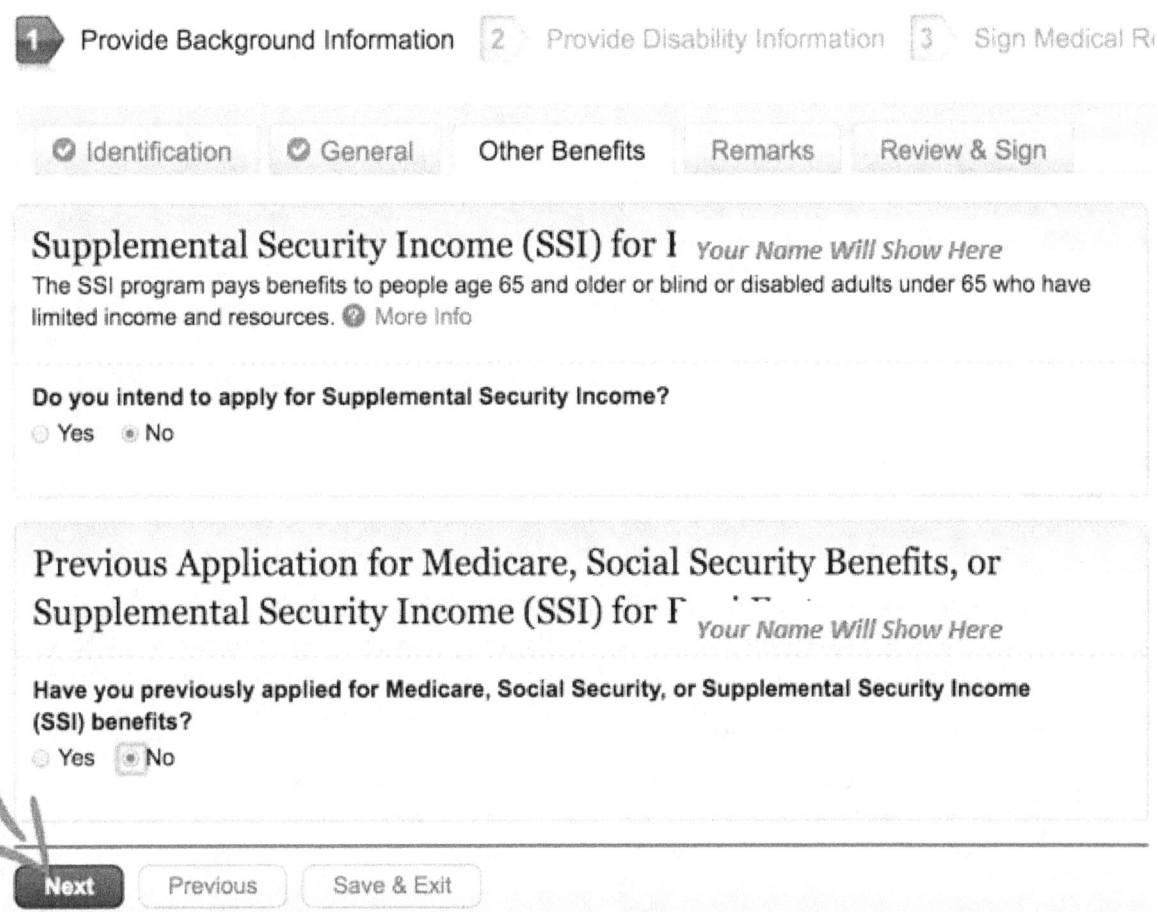

On this screen, you'll indicate whether you intend to apply for Supplemental Security Income.

Select "**Yes**" if you have limited income and resources **and** if either of these conditions apply:

1) You're 65 or older or
2) You're under the age of 65 and disabled or blind.

Note: "Limited income and resources" means that your countable monthly income doesn't exceed the Federal Benefit Rate (FBR). The monthly maximum Federal amounts for 2019 are $771 for an eligible individual, $1,157 for an eligible individual with an eligible spouse, and $386 for an essential person.

Example: An individual earning $825 per month from work would have $370 of countable income. This number is substantially lower than the federal benefit rate ($771), so the individual would be entitled to a SSI payment of $401.

Click the "**Next**" button to continue.

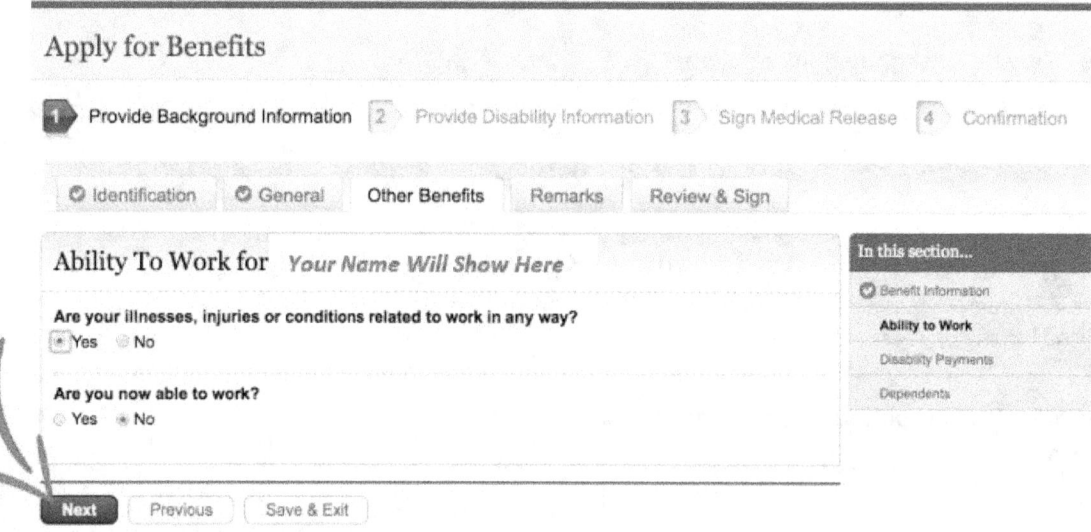

Here you'll indicate whether your illnesses, injuries, or conditions are related to your work in any way.

> **Example:** If you're a day laborer and you suffer from severe pain in your back, you would select "**Yes**" because it's likely that the physical nature of your occupation has taken a toll on your back and spine.

Then you'll indicate if you're now able to work.

 Warning: One of the main factors in deciding disability is whether you're able to perform "substantial gainful activity" (that is, whether you can work a basic full-time job). If you answered "**Yes**" on this last question, it's unlikely that your claim will be approved.

Click the "**Next**" button to continue.

Here you'll indicate whether <u>you've applied</u> or <u>intend to apply</u> for any workers' compensation or other public disability benefits.

 Note: If "**Yes**," your Social Security benefits may be reduced.

Note: If "**No**," you'll be asked to input a reason for not applying for other benefits.

Then you'll indicate whether you've received money from your employer on or after the date you became unable to work. If "**Yes**," you'll then input the amount of money and the type of money.

   Examples: Sick pay, vacation pay, severance pay, etc.

Lastly, you'll indicate whether you expect to receive any money from your employer in the future. If "**Yes**," you'll then input the amount of money and the type of money.

   Examples: Sick pay, vacation pay, severance pay, etc.

Click the "**Next**" button to continue.

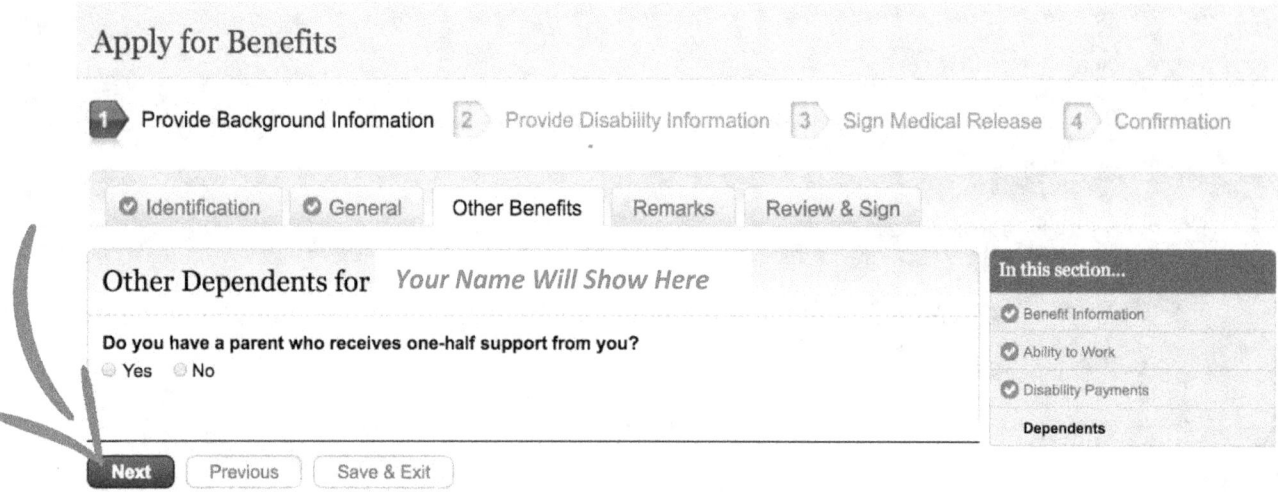

Here you'll indicate whether you have a parent who receives one-half support from you.

Click the "**Next**" button to continue.

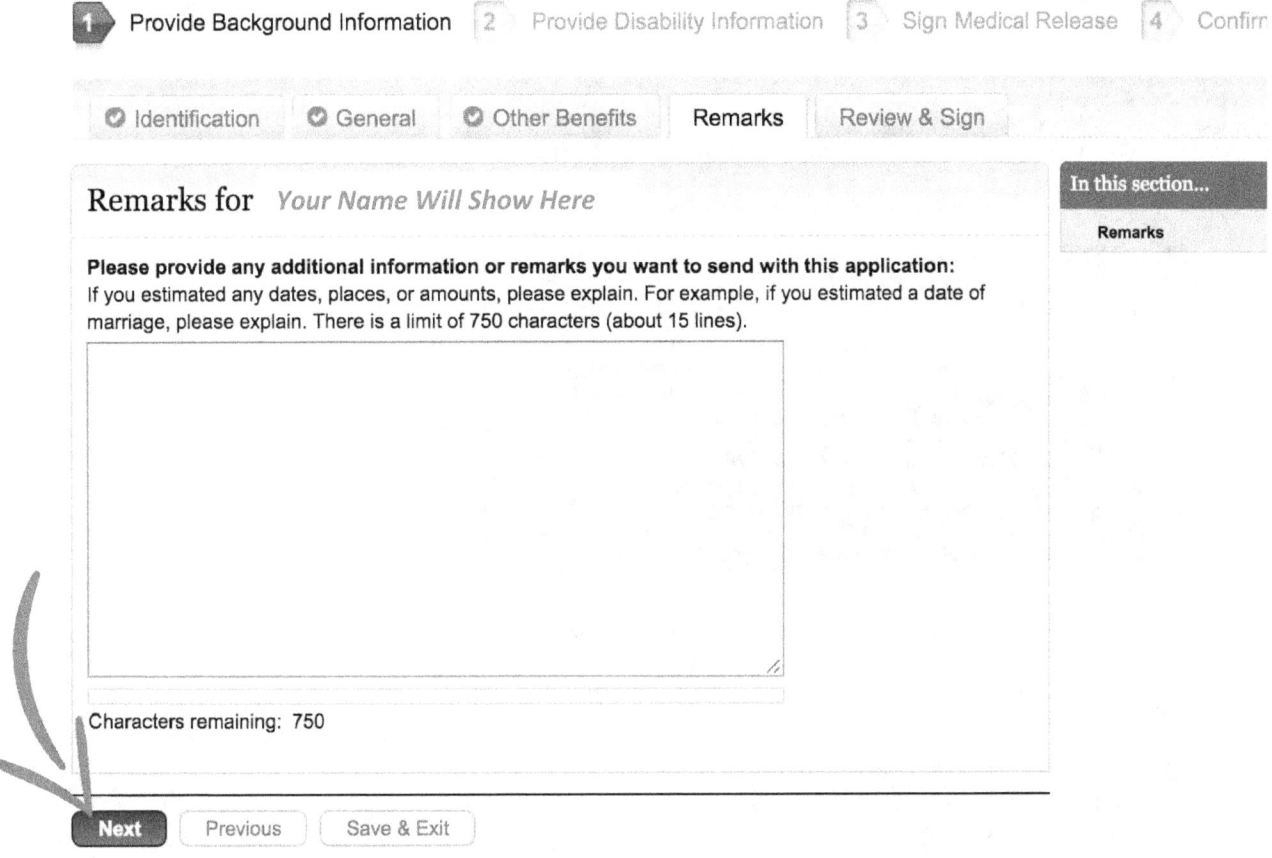

On this screen, you may input any "**Remarks**" or comments that you wish to include in your application. This is the perfect place to indicate whether you're uncertain about any of your prior responses. You can also use this space to let SSA know of any unique circumstances regarding your background information.

 Note: Don't include any information about your disability(ies) here. You'll have an opportunity to do so in Step 2 of the application process.

Click the "**Next**" button to review your information and to electronically sign-off on this section of your application.

 **Need a break?** By this point, you've probably been working on your application for about an hour, and it may be a good time to click the "**Save & Exit**" button to rest your eyes and your brain. If you take a break now, you can review your information when you're feeling rested and your eyes are fresh, which will help you ensure the accuracy of your answers before moving on to the next section.

Return to Your Saved Application

You can return to a saved application here anytime: https://www.ssa.gov/benefits/disability

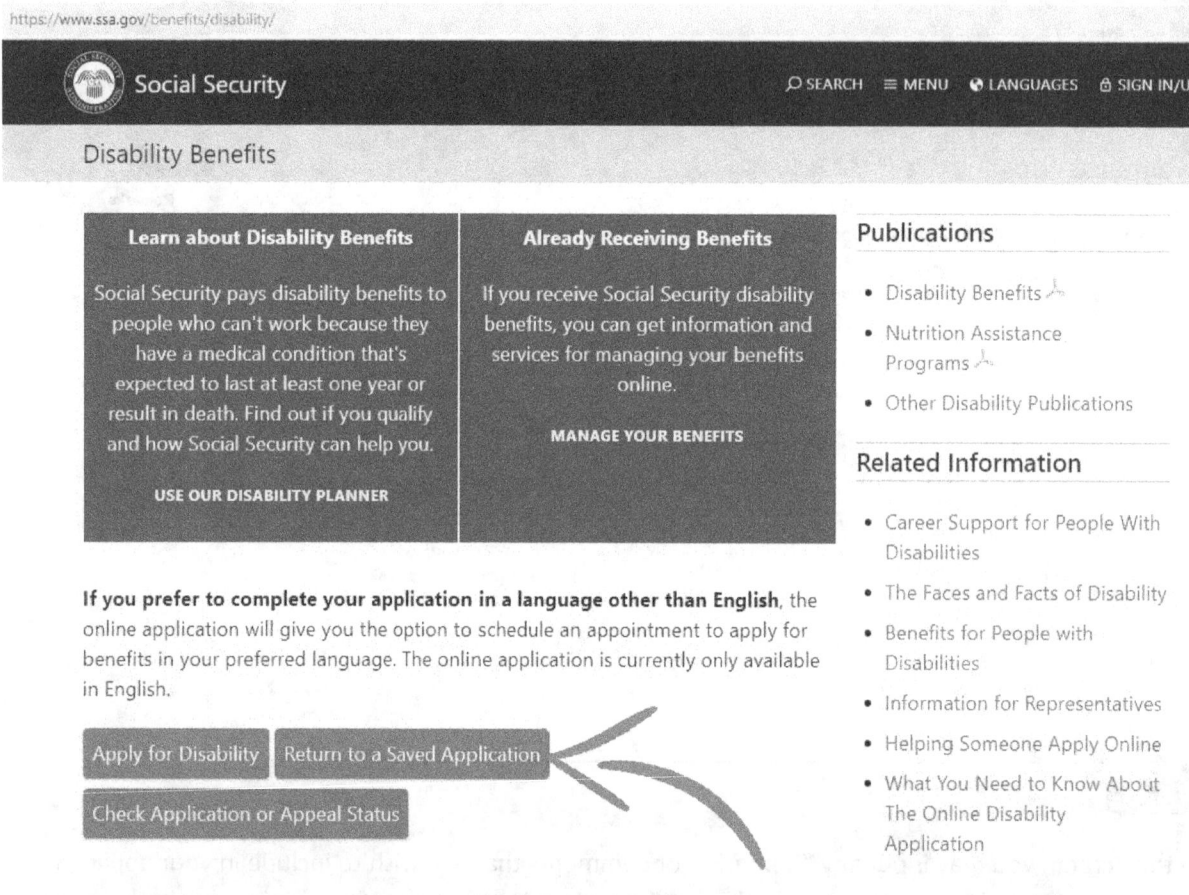

You may also log into your *my* Social Security account to return to your saved application.

Then you must agree to the terms of service.

Apply for Benefits

Benefits Application Terms of Service

I understand that I am entering a U.S. Government System to file a benefit application with the Social Security Administration. I understand that I need to provide the Social Security Administration information to process the benefit application. I understand that failing to agree to the statements below will result in my inability to file a benefit application online, which may prevent the Social Security Administration from making an accurate and timely decision about eligibility for benefits.

I understand that:

- the Social Security Administration will validate the information I provide against the information in Social Security Administration's systems.
- my activities may be monitored within this site.
- any person who knowingly and willfully tries to obtain Social Security benefits falsely could be punished by a fine or imprisonment, or both.
- I am authorized to file a claim on my own behalf or on behalf of someone else with the Social Security Administration.

Information about Social Security's Online Policies

The privacy of our customers is always very important to us. We encourage you to read our Privacy Act Statement.

☑ **I understand and agree to the above statements.**

[Next]   [Exit]

Click the "**Next**" button to continue.

Click the "**Return to Saved Application Process**" button.

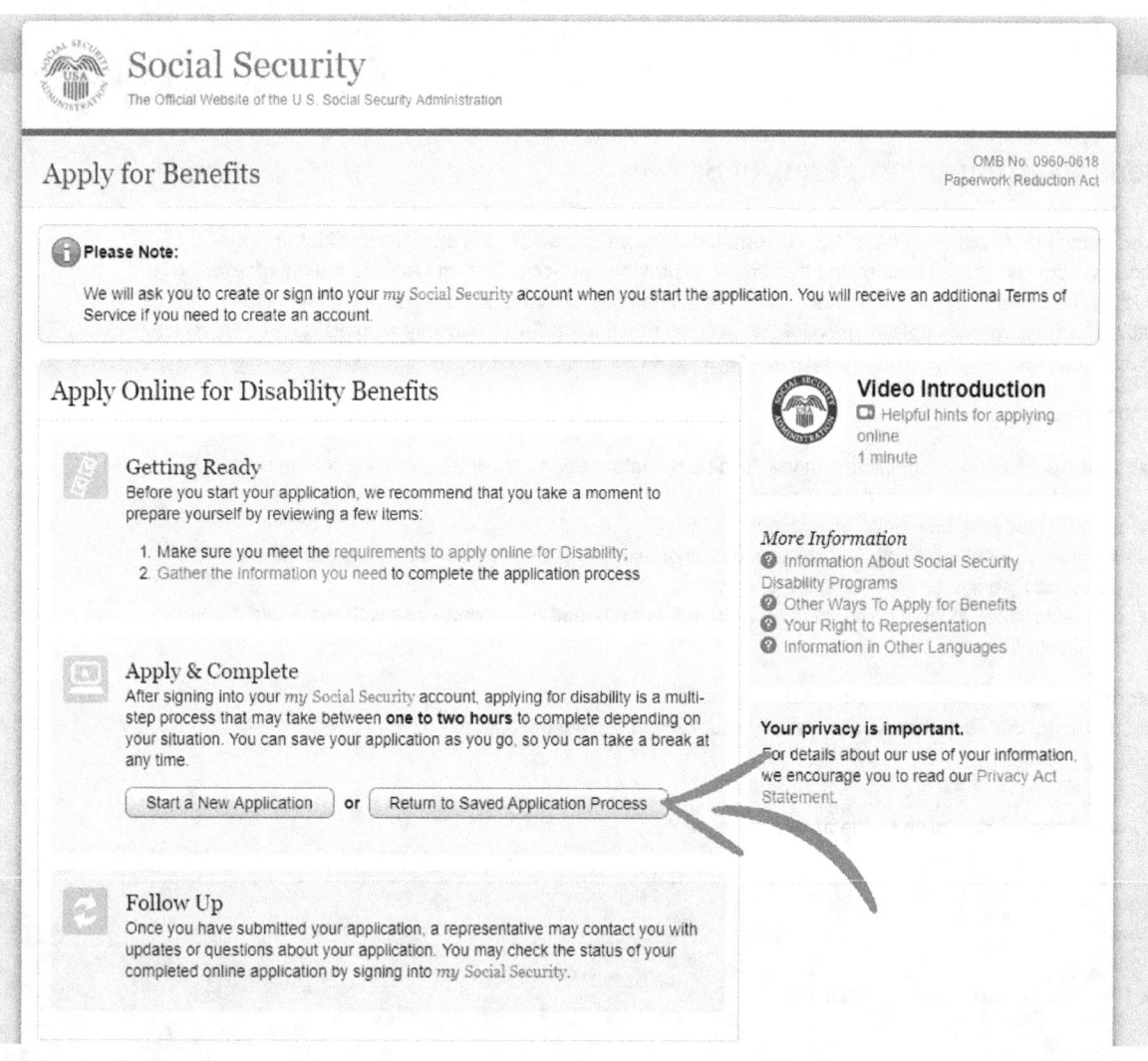

Next, input your Social Security Number and your Re-entry Number.

Apply for Benefits

Return to Saved Application Process
Provide Re-entry Number and the Social Security Number to continue where you left off.

Applicant's Social Security Number (SSN):

Re-entry Number: Forgot or lost Re-entry Number

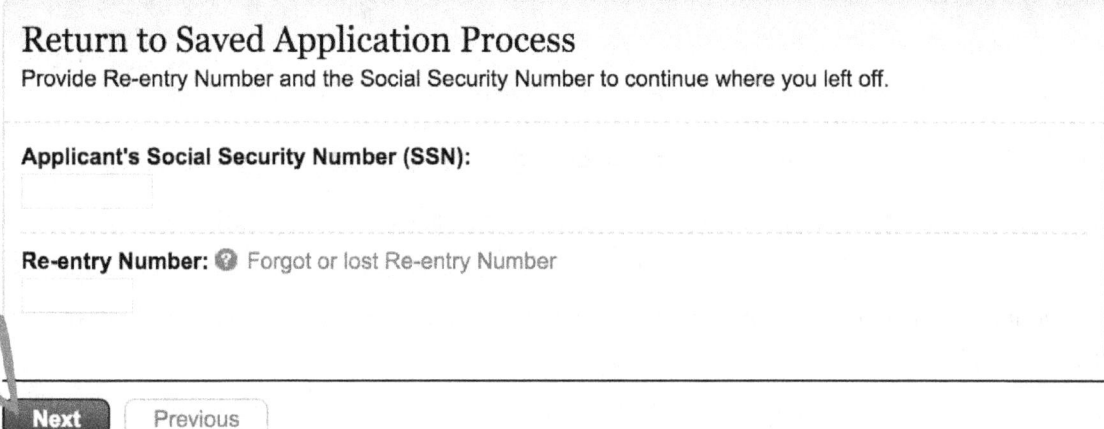

Click the "**Next**" button to continue.

Apply for Benefits

1 Provide Background Information | **2** Provide Disability Information | **3** Sign Medical Release | **4** Confirmation

Identification | General | Other Benefits | Remarks | **Review & Sign**

Review Information for *Your Name Will Show Here*
If you need to make any changes, please select the "Edit" button to return to that page.

In this section...
Overall Summary

This section will display all the information you provided in the "Background Information" section.

Review all information carefully. If you see any mistakes, you can click on the appropriate tab above to go backward into your application. You can also click on the "**Previous**" button at the bottom.

Once you've double-checked your information, you must review and accept the "**Electronic Signature Agreement**."

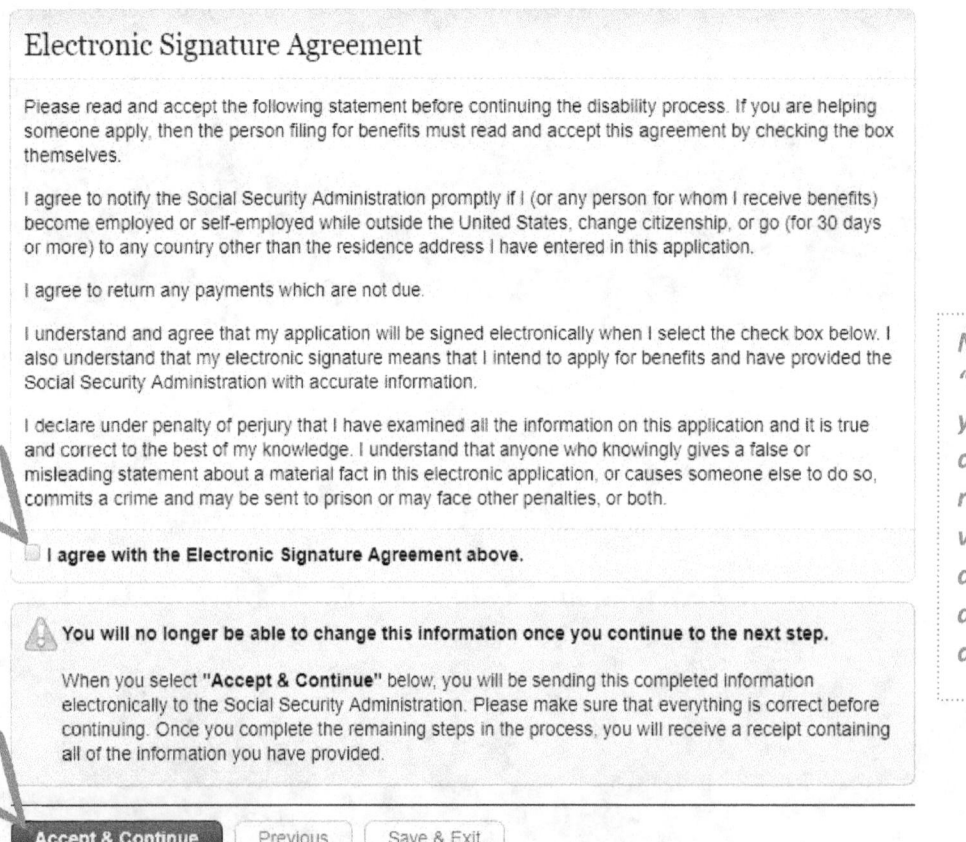

Note: Once you click the "Accept & Continue" button, you won't be able to make any changes to your responses in Step 1. So it's very important that you answer questions truthfully and to the best of your ability before proceeding.

When ready, check the "**I agree...**" box, then click the "**Accept & Continue**" button to proceed to Step 2.

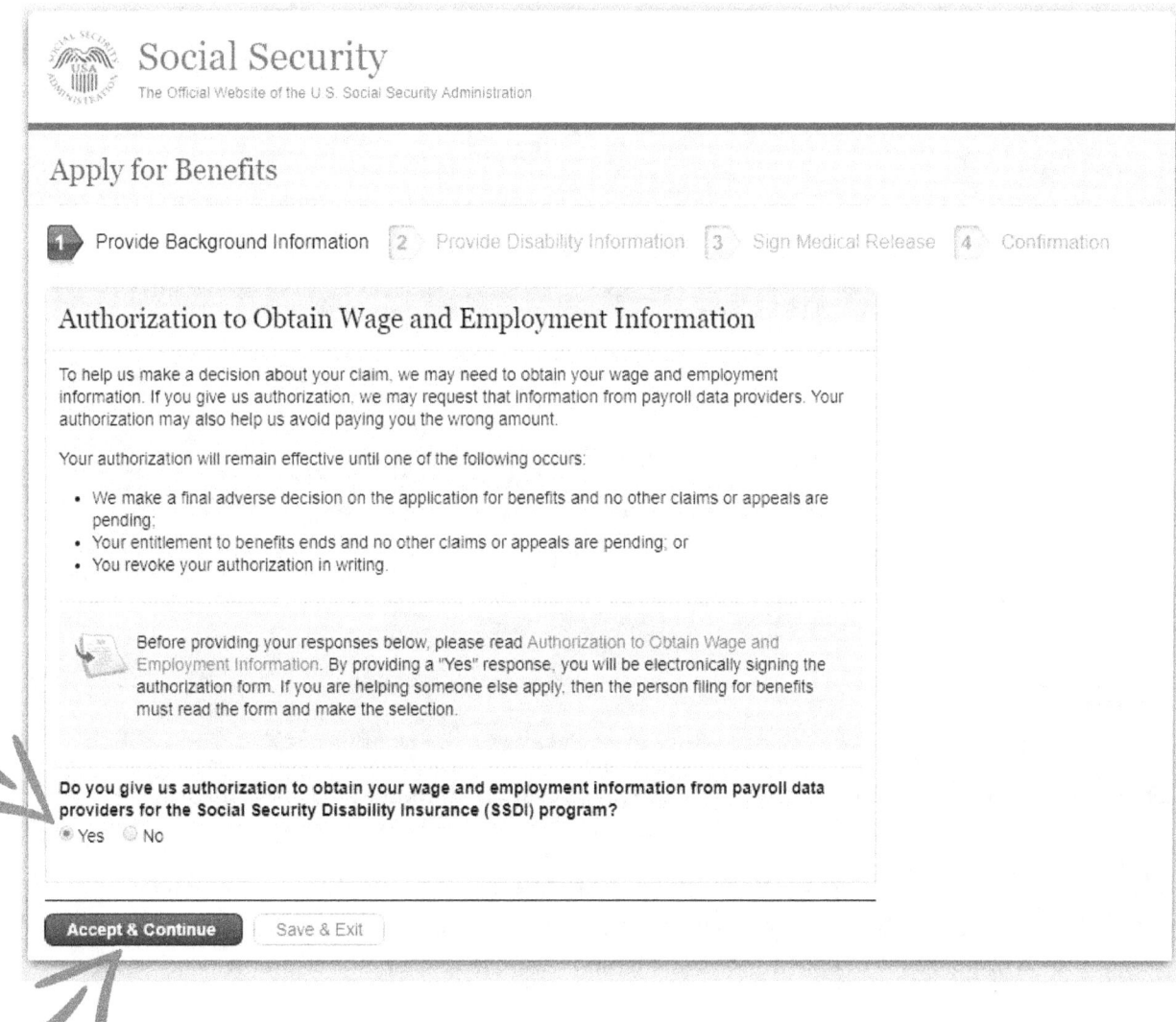

On this screen, you'll give SSA permission to obtain your wage and employment information from payroll data.

Select "**Yes**" if you agree and click the "**Accept & Continue**" button.

Here you can download the "**Authorization Scope and Duration Statement**" for your records.

Note: This authorization remains in effect until: (1) Your application(s) is denied in a final decision and no other claims or appeals are pending; (2) Your entitlement for SSDI benefits ends and no other claims or appeals are pending; (3) You revoke your authorization in writing.

Click the "**Next**" button to continue.

Way to go!!

You've finished Step 1 of 4 of the application process.

You're now on Step 2.

Step 2: Provide Disability Information

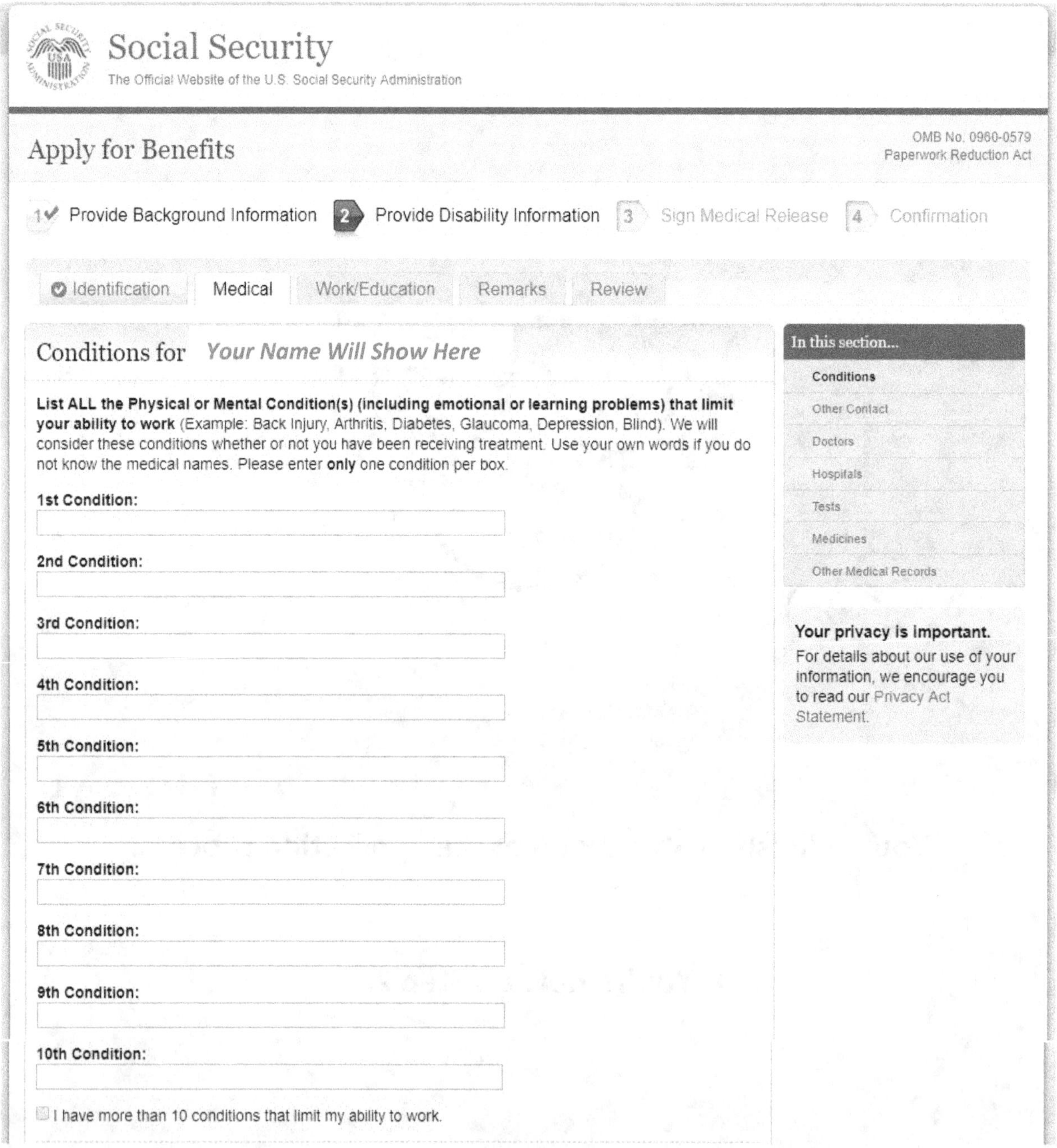

[Screenshot of Social Security "Apply for Benefits" online form, Step 2: Provide Disability Information, Medical tab. Shows "Conditions for Your Name Will Show Here" with instructions: "List ALL the Physical or Mental Condition(s) (including emotional or learning problems) that limit your ability to work (Example: Back Injury, Arthritis, Diabetes, Glaucoma, Depression, Blind). We will consider these conditions whether or not you have been receiving treatment. Use your own words if you do not know the medical names. Please enter only one condition per box." Form fields for 1st through 10th Condition, with checkbox "I have more than 10 conditions that limit my ability to work." Sidebar lists: Conditions, Other Contact, Doctors, Hospitals, Tests, Medicines, Other Medical Records. Privacy notice included.]

Here you'll input your various conditions. They may be physical or mental conditions.

Note: I recommend that to put the most serious condition(s) first and second, followed by the rest of your conditions.

Note: Don't be shy! Be sure to include anything and everything that causes you pain, discomfort, anguish, anxiety, or the like.

(Screen Continued)

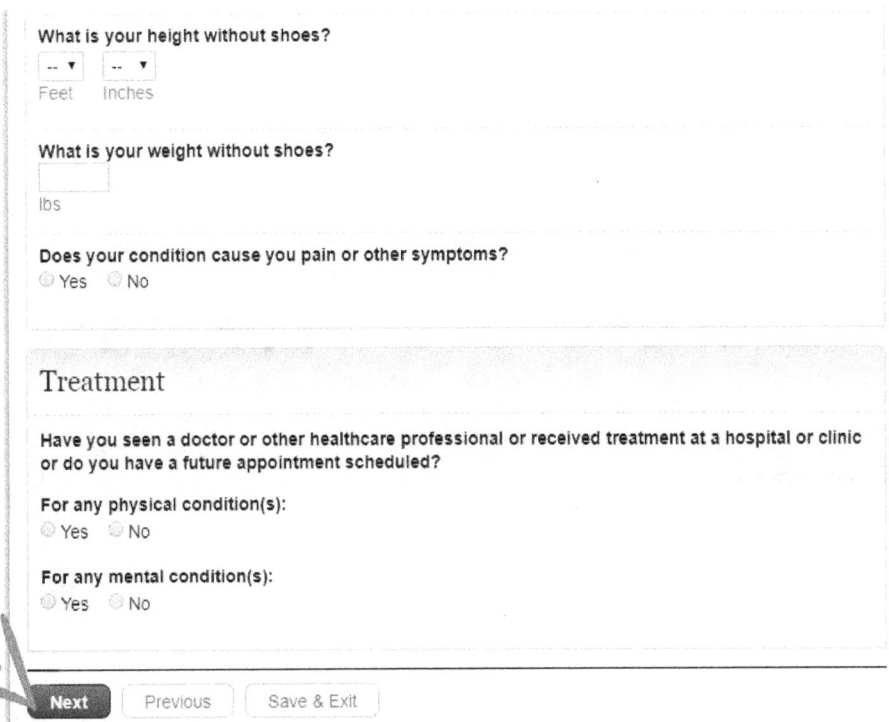

Input your height and weight (without shoes), and state whether your condition causes you pain or other symptoms.

Lastly, indicate whether you've been seen by a doctor or other healthcare professional or received treatment at a hospital or clinic OR if you have a future appointment scheduled for:

- Physical condition(s) or
- Mental condition(s).

Select "**Yes**" for whichever condition(s) apply.

Click the "**Next**" button to continue.

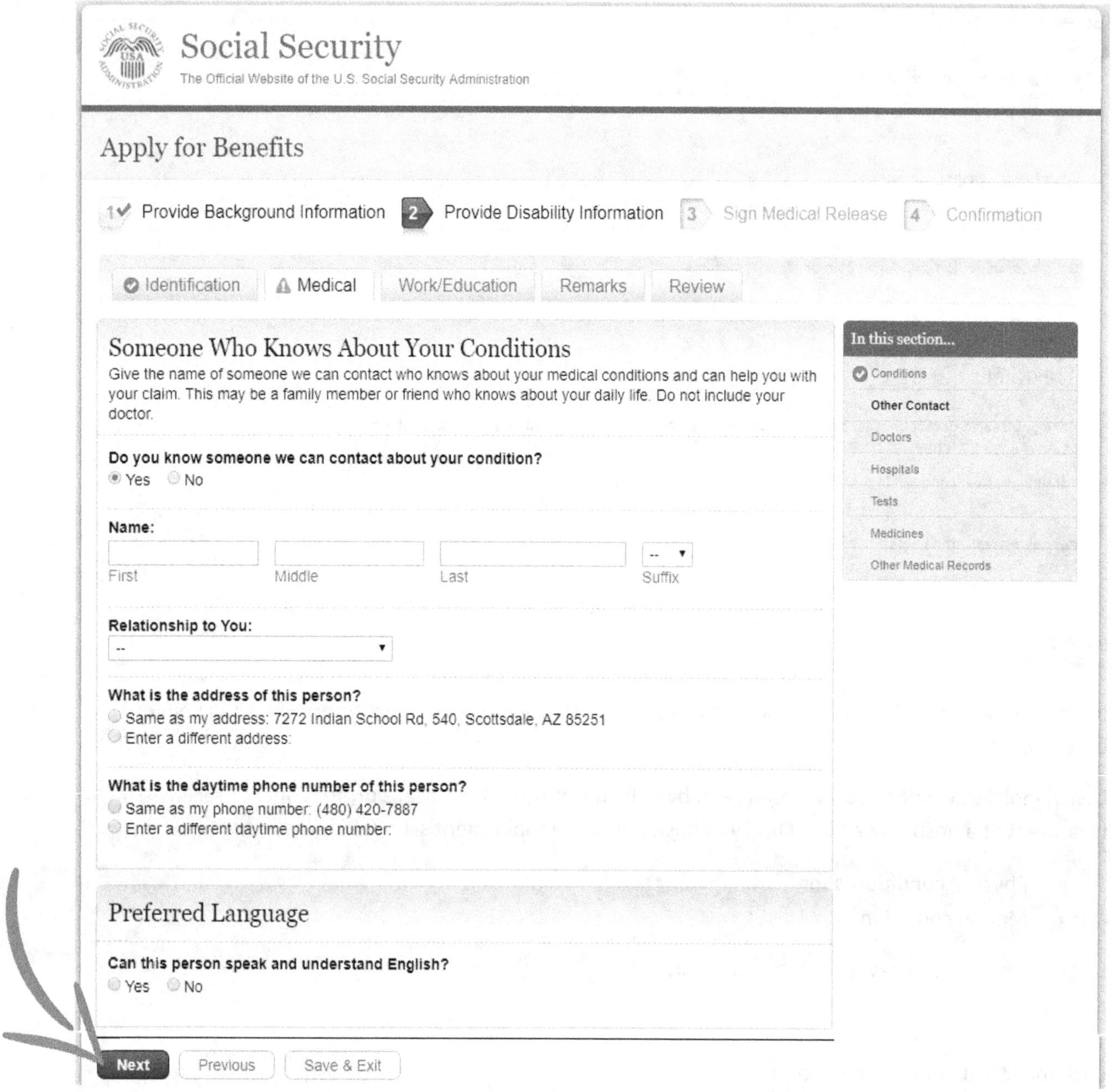

Indicate whether you know someone SSA can contact about your condition(s).

This might include a spouse, a child, a friend, a co-worker, a nurse or doctor, a caretaker, or some other individual with firsthand personal knowledge of your condition(s).

Note: I suggest that you to select "**Yes**" and input the name of a person who knows you and who is willing to communicate with SSA about their observations of your condition(s). If "**Yes**," input the contact information of the individual.

Click the "**Next**" button to continue.

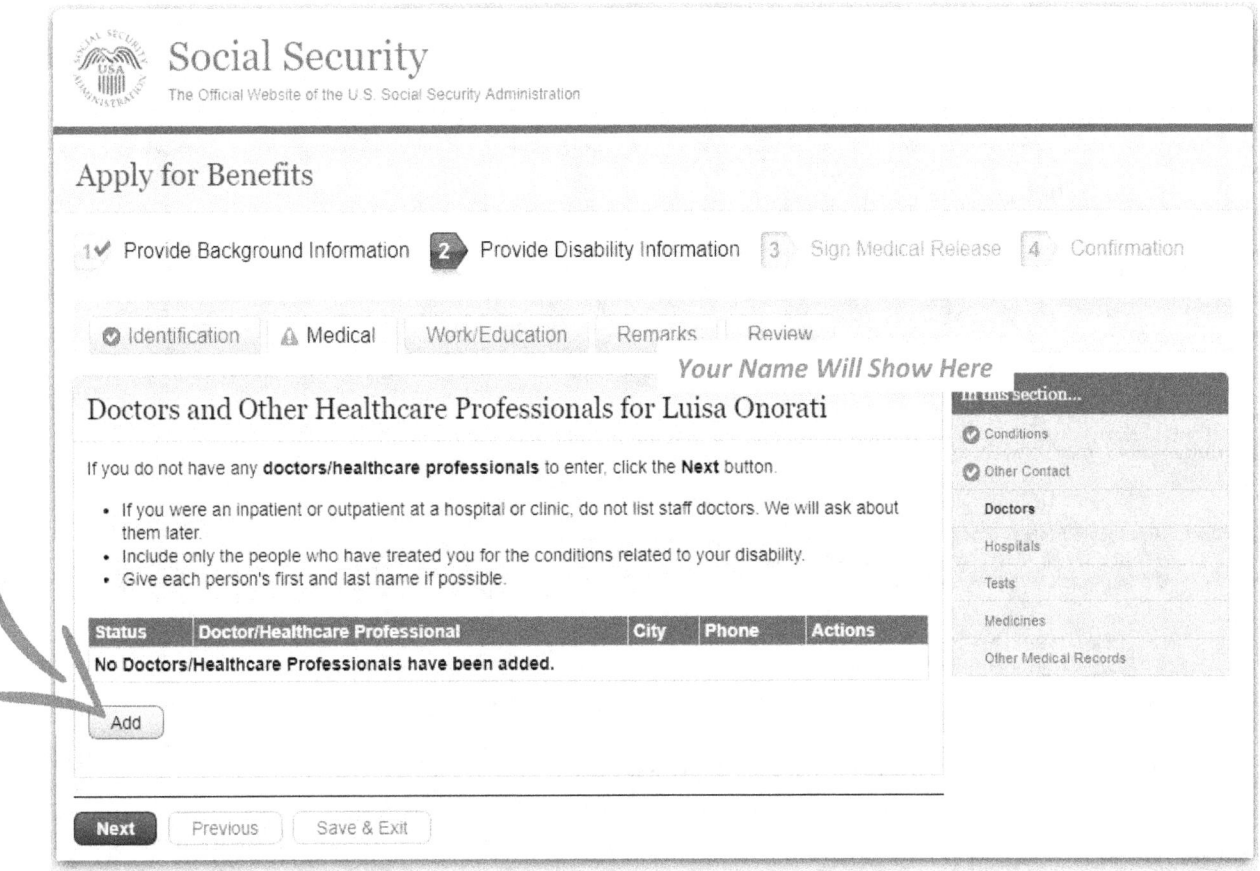

Here you'll add the **Doctors and/or Healthcare Professionals** who have treated you.

Click the "**Add**" button to add a doctor and/or a healthcare professional.

Add New Doctor/Healthcare Professional   (Screen 1 of 3)

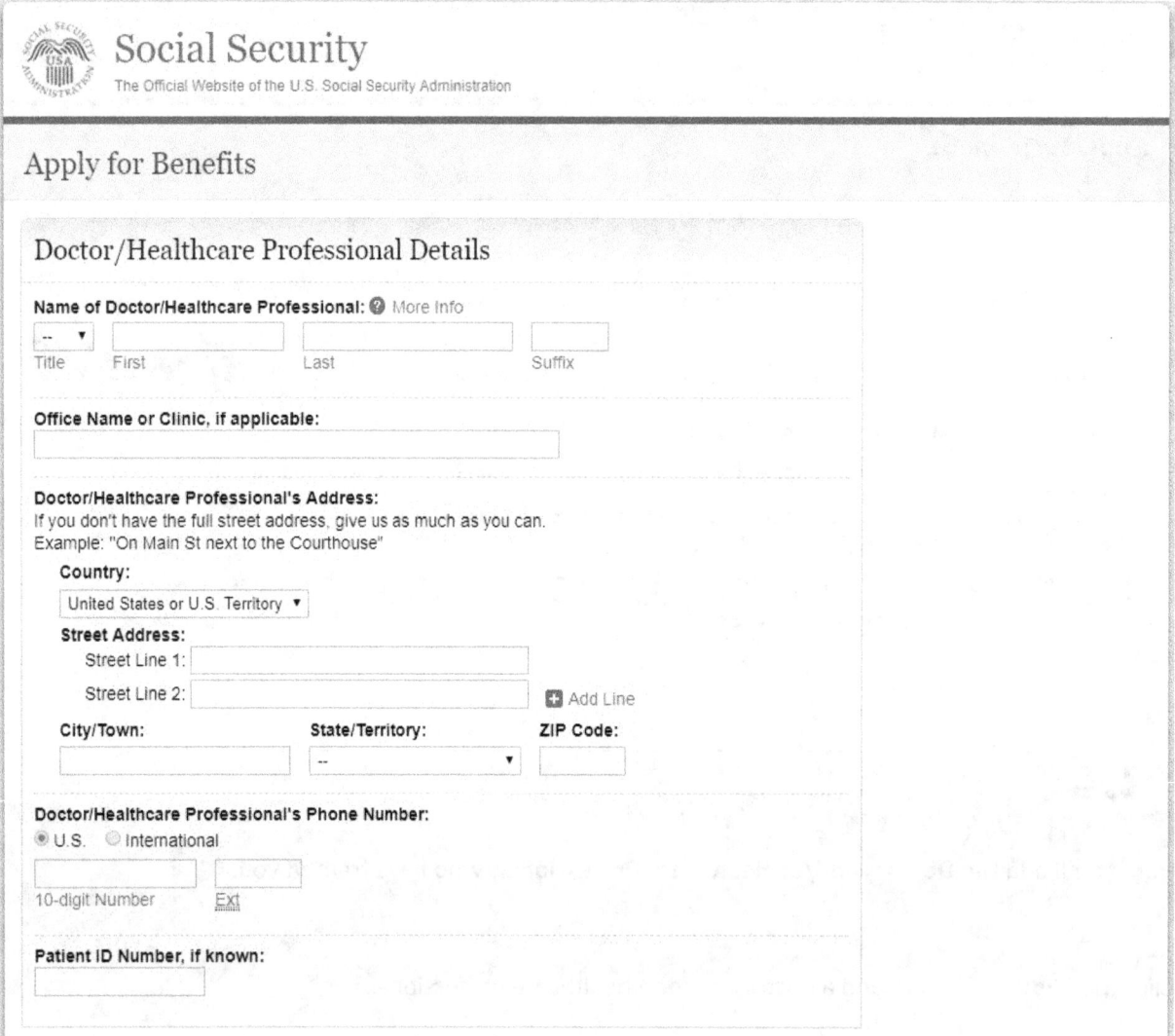

On this part of the screen, input the name of your doctor and/or healthcare professional, the office or clinic name (if applicable), the address, the phone number, and the patient ID number (if known).

Add New Doctor/Healthcare Professional (Screen 2 of 3)

> **Treatment Dates with this Doctor/Healthcare Professional**
> Please give us the closest date(s) you can remember. ● More Info
>
> **First visit:**
>
> **Last visit:**
>
> **Next visit:**
> Leave blank if no appointment scheduled.

> **Tests Ordered by this Doctor/Healthcare Professional**
> ● More Info
>
> **Has this doctor/healthcare professional ordered any tests for you?**
> This includes any medical tests you have had or will have.
> ○ Yes ○ No

> **Medicines Recommended or Prescribed by this Doctor/Healthcare Professional**
>
> **Has this doctor/healthcare professional recommended or prescribed any medicines for you?**
> ○ Yes ○ No

On this part of the screen, input:

Treatment Dates:

- First visit (feel free to approximate)
- Last visit (feel free to approximate)
- Next visit (even if it's unscheduled).

Tests Ordered:

Input the kind of test(s) ordered and the date(s) ordered (e.g., EKG, MRIs, X-rays, etc.).

Medicines Recommended or Prescribed:

Input the names of the medicine(s) this doctor or provider prescribed and the reason the medicine was prescribed.

Add New Doctor/Healthcare Professional   (Screen 3 of 3)

> **Medical Conditions Treated by this Doctor/Healthcare Professional**
>
> What medical conditions were treated or evaluated by this doctor/healthcare professional?
> Examples: back injury, arthritis, diabetes, depression, blind. (1000 characters maximum)
>
> [text box]
>
> Characters remaining: 1000
>
> **Treatment from this Doctor/Healthcare Professional**
>
> What treatment did you receive from this doctor/healthcare professional?
> You DO NOT need to repeat any information that you have already told us about medicines and tests. Examples of treatment: examinations, regular evaluations, check ups, physical therapy, chemotherapy, counseling. (1000 character maximum)
>
> [text box]
>
> Characters remaining: 1000
>
> [Save] [Cancel]

On this part of the screen, input:

Medical Conditions Treated by This Doctor or Healthcare Professional:

> Input all the conditions, injuries, or other ailments treated by this doctor or healthcare professional.

Treatment from This Doctor or Healthcare Professional:

> Input the treatment you received from this doctor or healthcare professional.

Click the "**Save**" button to save all data and return to the main "Medical" tab.

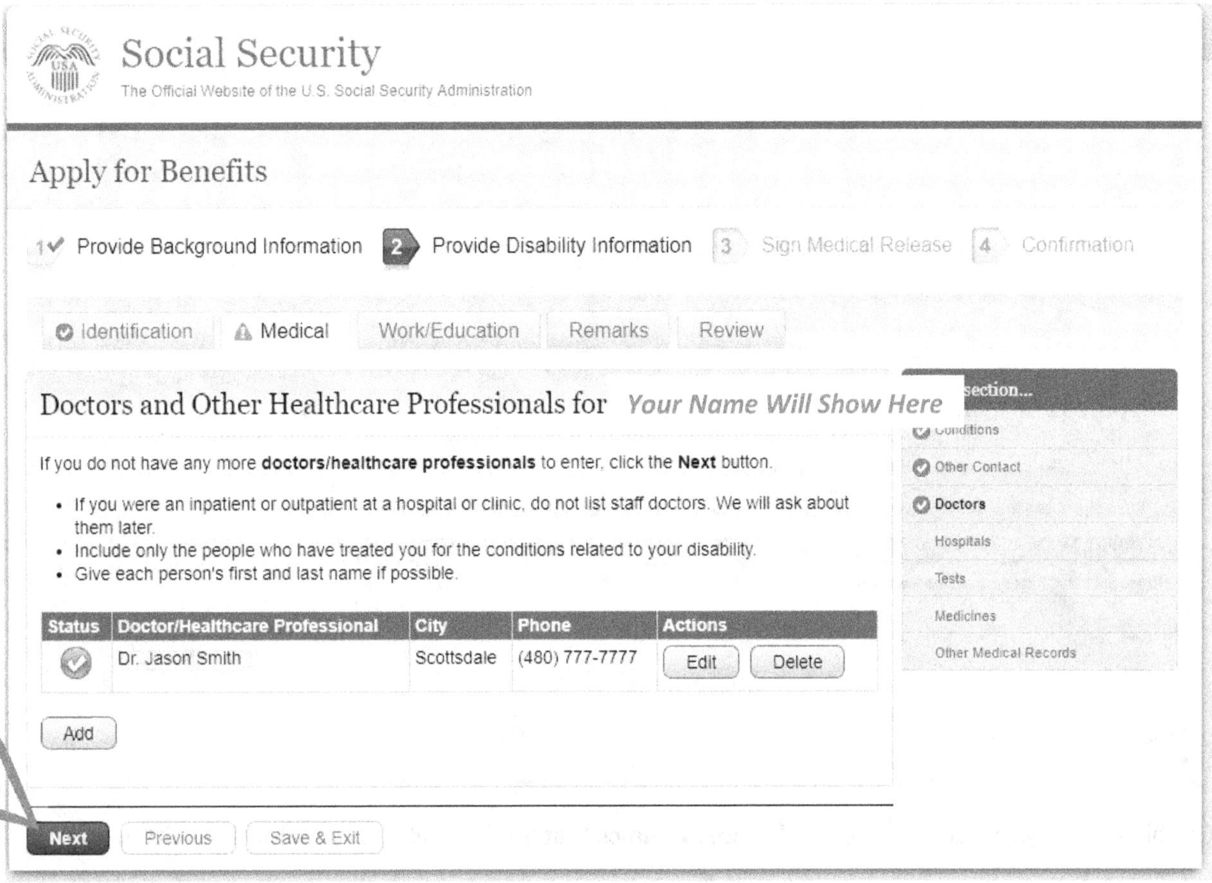

Note: You'll see the doctor's name and information you just added in the "Status" table.

Click the "**Add**" button to add another doctor or healthcare professional, until you've added all the doctors or healthcare professionals you've visited.

Note: Be sure to add all your doctors and healthcare providers! Try not to leave anything out, but if you happen to forget someone, you can always add a doctor or healthcare provider later.

Click the "**Next**" button to continue.

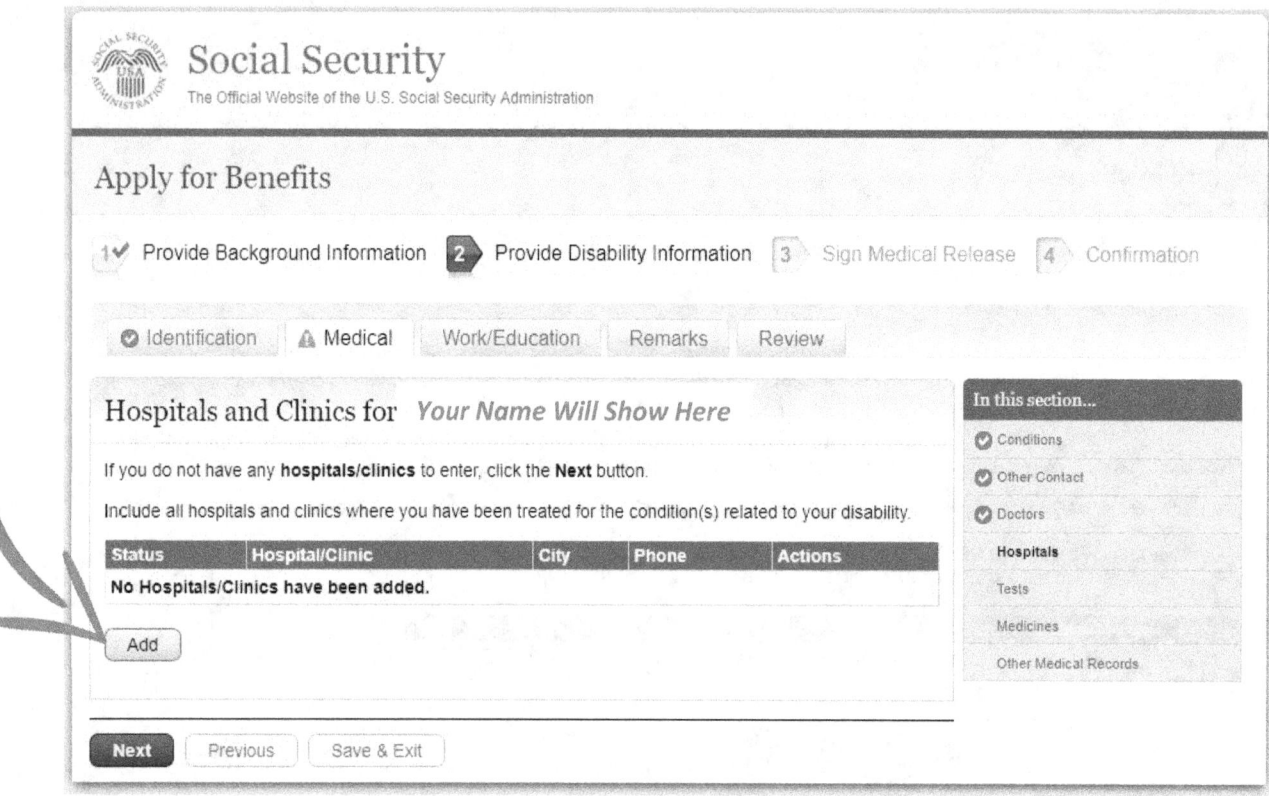

On this screen, you'll add the **Hospitals and/or Clinics** that you've visited or that have admitted you.

Click the "**Add**" button to add a new hospital and/or clinic.

Note: You'll input details similar to those you just added for your doctors and healthcare providers. Continue to add new hospitals and clinics (including urgent care clinics) until you're finished.

Click the "**Next**" button to continue.

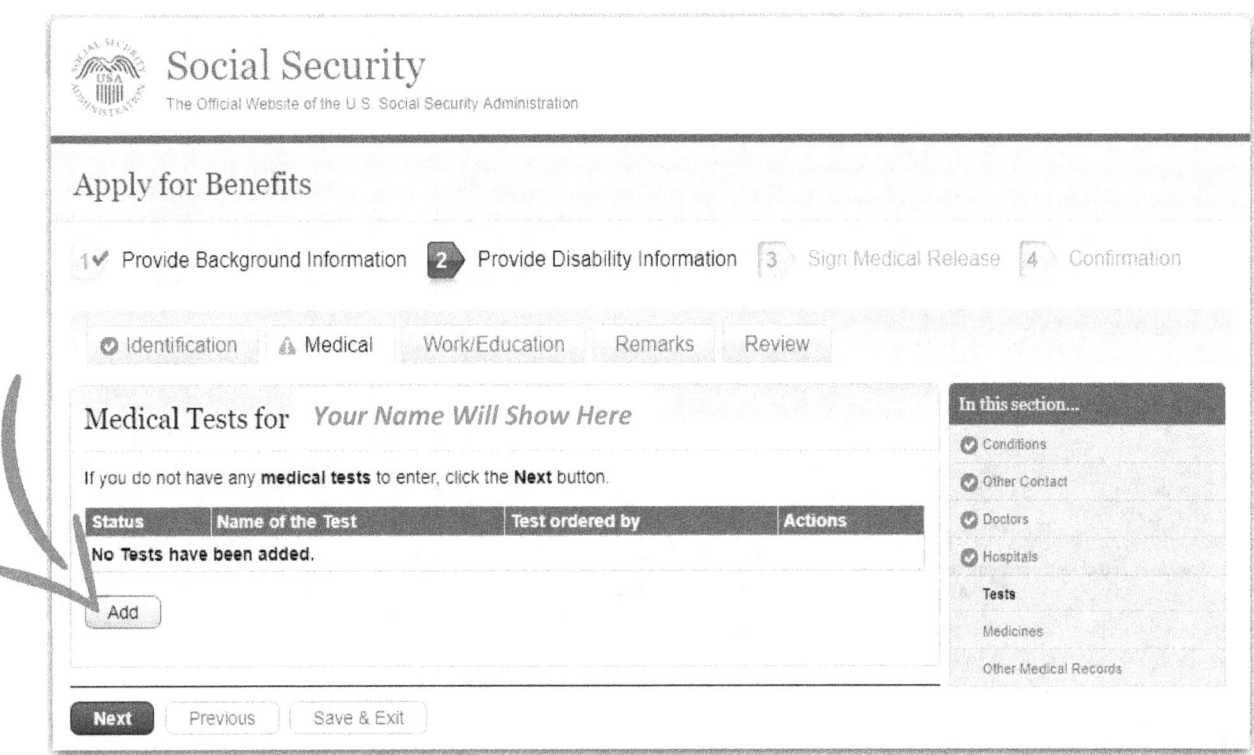

On this screen, you'll add any **Medical Tests** you've undergone.

Click the "**Add**" button to add a new medical test.

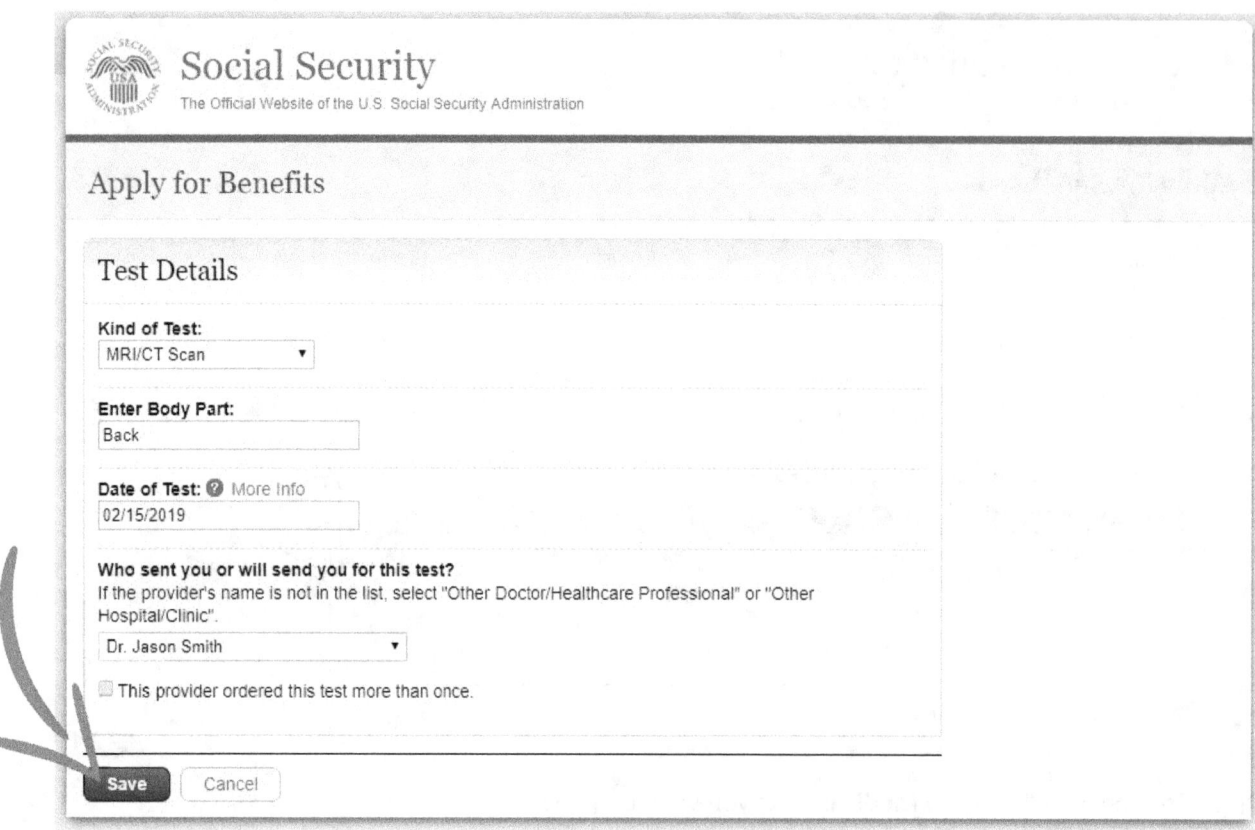

On this screen, input details of any **Medical Test** you've undergone.

1) Indicate the **Kind of Test** from the drop-down menu.
2) Enter the **Body Part** that was subjected to the test.
3) Input the **Date of Test.**
4) Select the doctor or healthcare provider who ordered the test.
5) Indicate whether that doctor or healthcare provider ordered this test more than once.

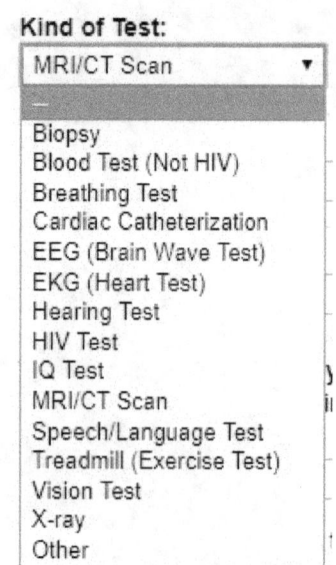

Click the "**Save**" button to save the Medical Test data, then return to the main "Medical Tests" screen.

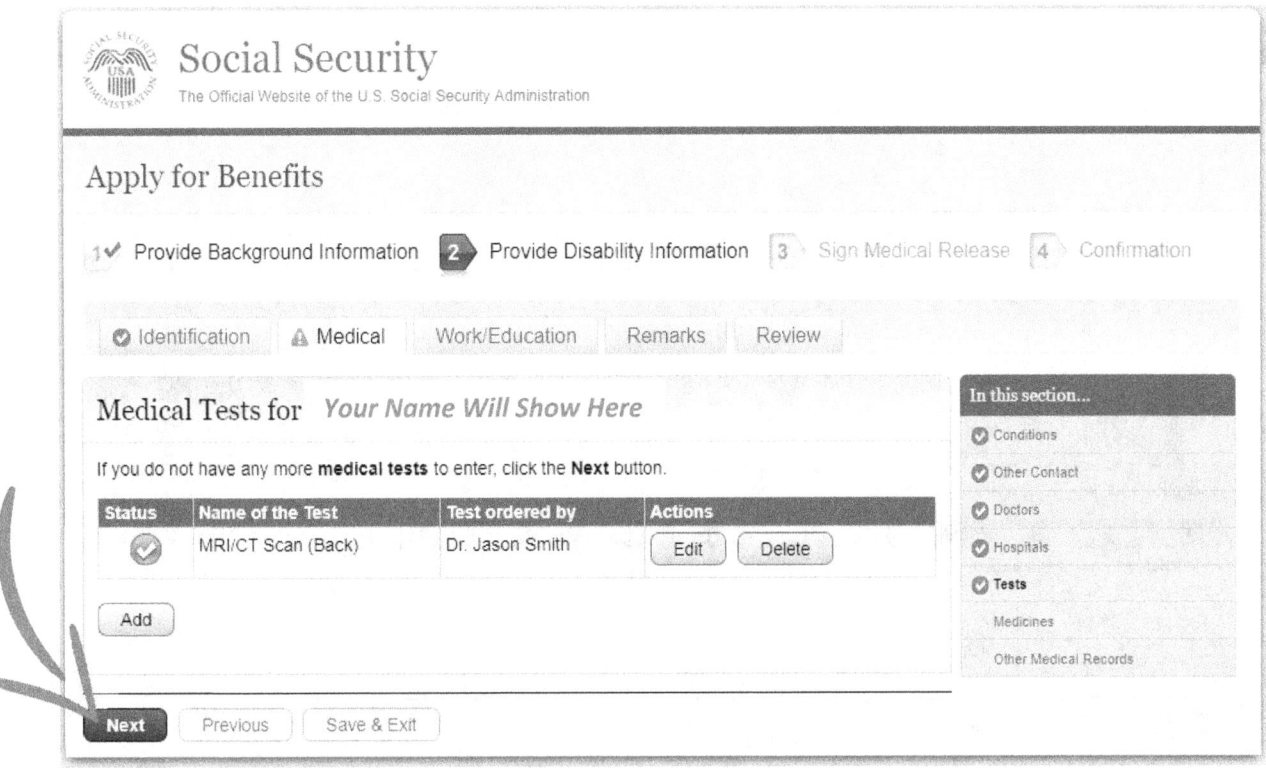

On this screen, you'll see the Medical Tests you just added.

You can always click the "**Edit**" button to modify the test or the "**Delete**" button to remove the test from the table.

Continue to add new Medical Tests until you're finished.

Click the "**Next**" button to continue.

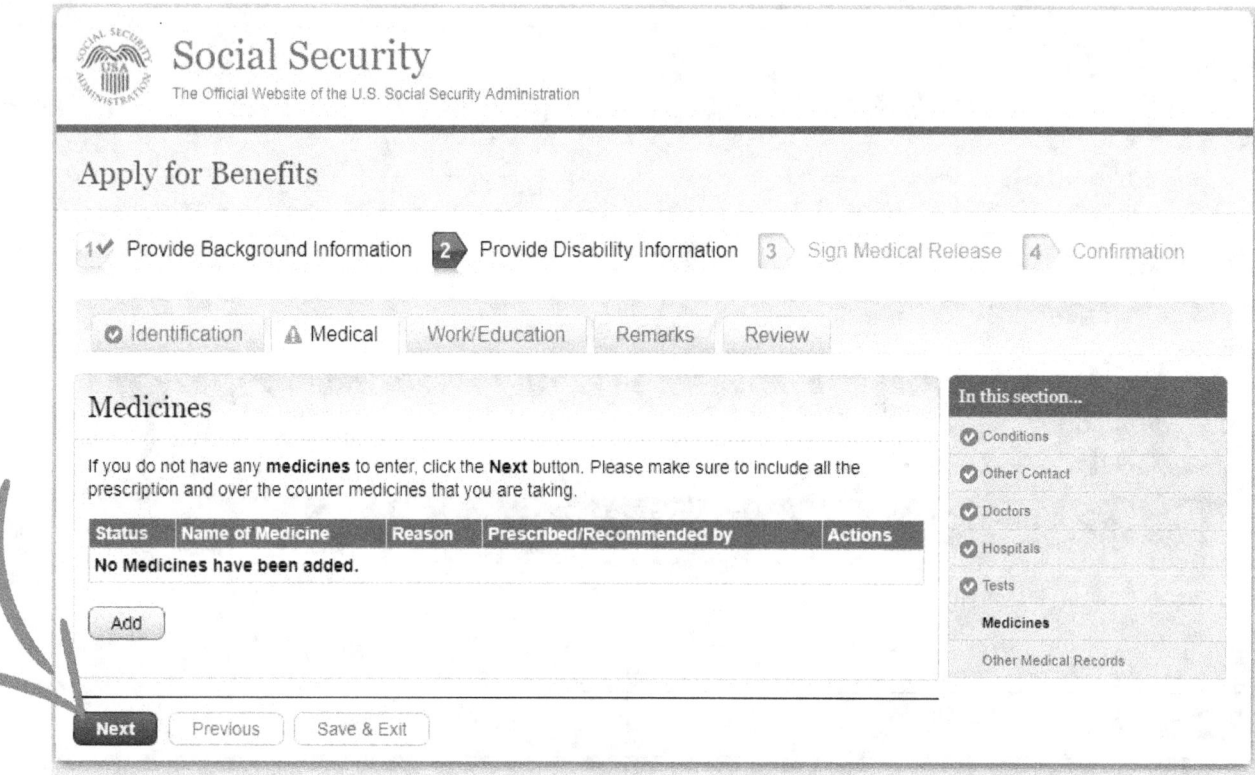

On this screen, add any and all Medicines you're taking.

Click the "**Add**" button to add new Medicines.

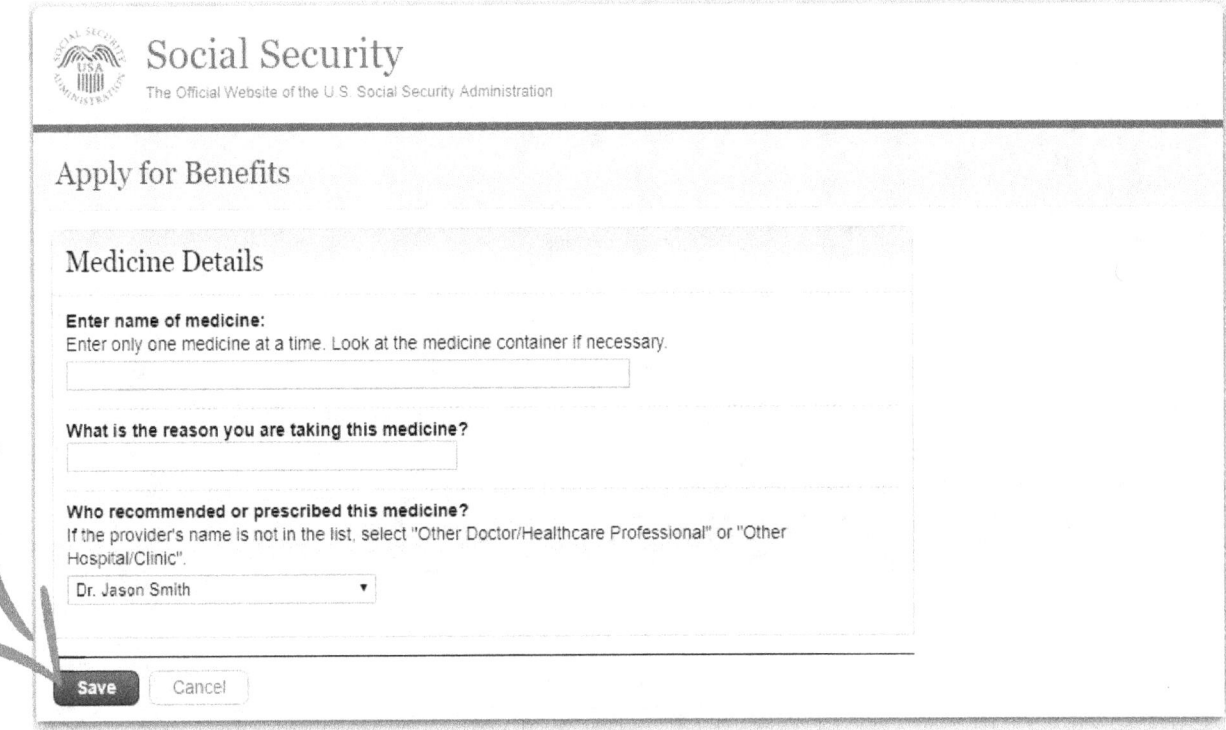

On this screen, input details of any Medicines you're taking.

1. Enter the name of medicines (one at a time).
2. Input the reason you're taking this medicine.
3. Select from the drop-down menu the name of the doctor or healthcare professional who recommended or prescribed this medicine.

Click the "**Save**" button to save the Medicine Details data, then return to the main "Medicines" screen.

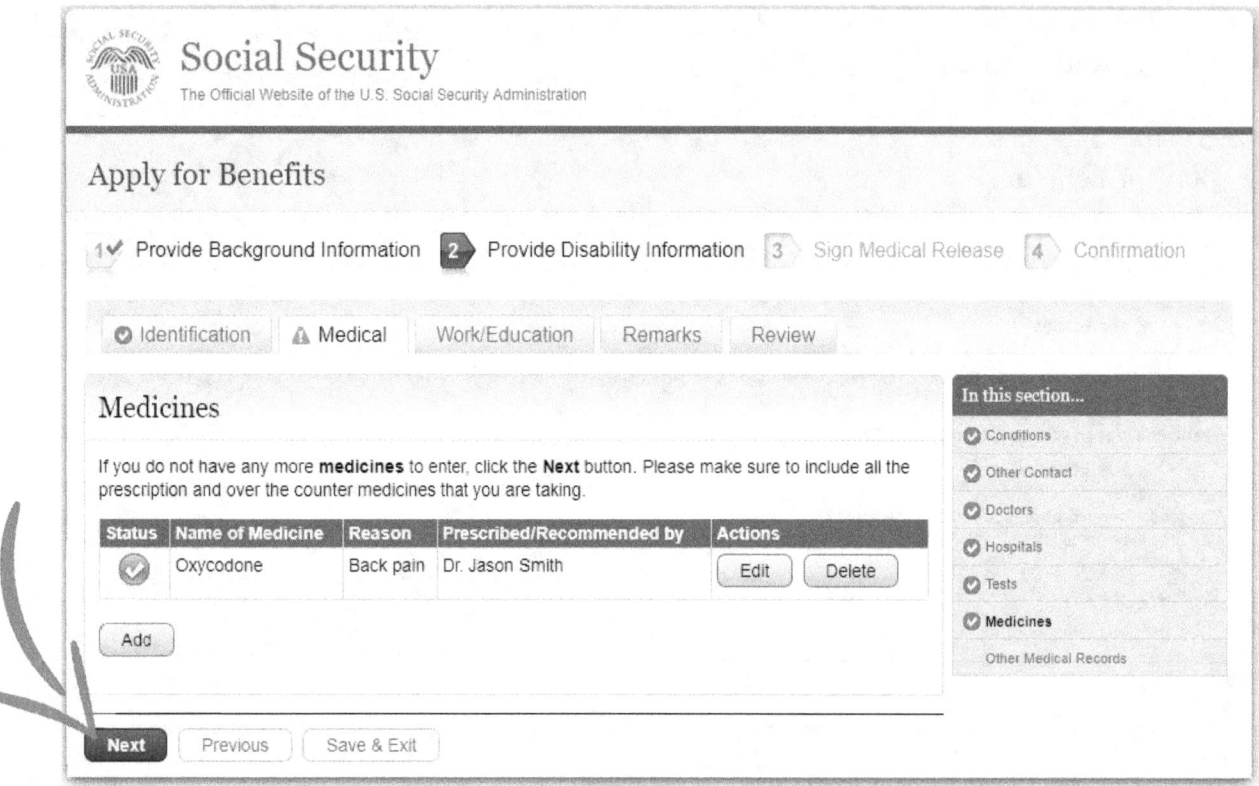

On this page, you'll see the Medicines you just added.

You can always click the "**Edit**" button to modify a medicine or the "**Delete**" button to remove a medicine from the table.

Continue to add new medicines until you're finished.

Click the "**Next**" button to continue to the "Other Medical Records" page.

On this screen, you can add Other Medical Records.

Click the "**Add**" button to add a new Medical Record.

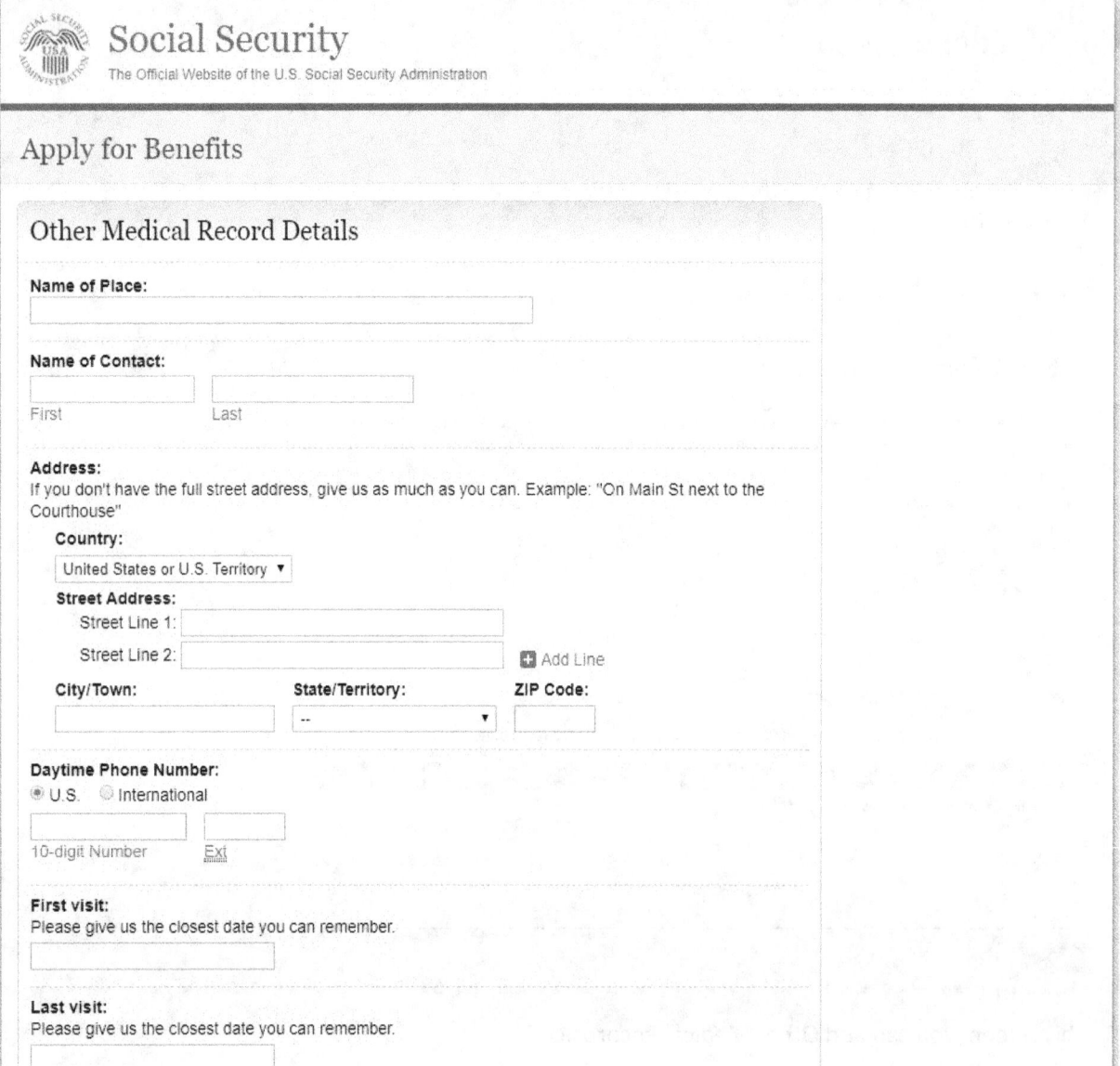

Input the details regarding Other Medical Records.

Examples include:

- Vocational rehabilitation services
- Workers compensation
- FMLA
- Public welfare
- Prison or jail records
- Military or VA medical records
- Records held by an attorney or lawyer
- Medical records in another place (other).

Click the "**Save**" button to save the Other Medical Record Details data, then return to the main "Other Medical Records" screen.

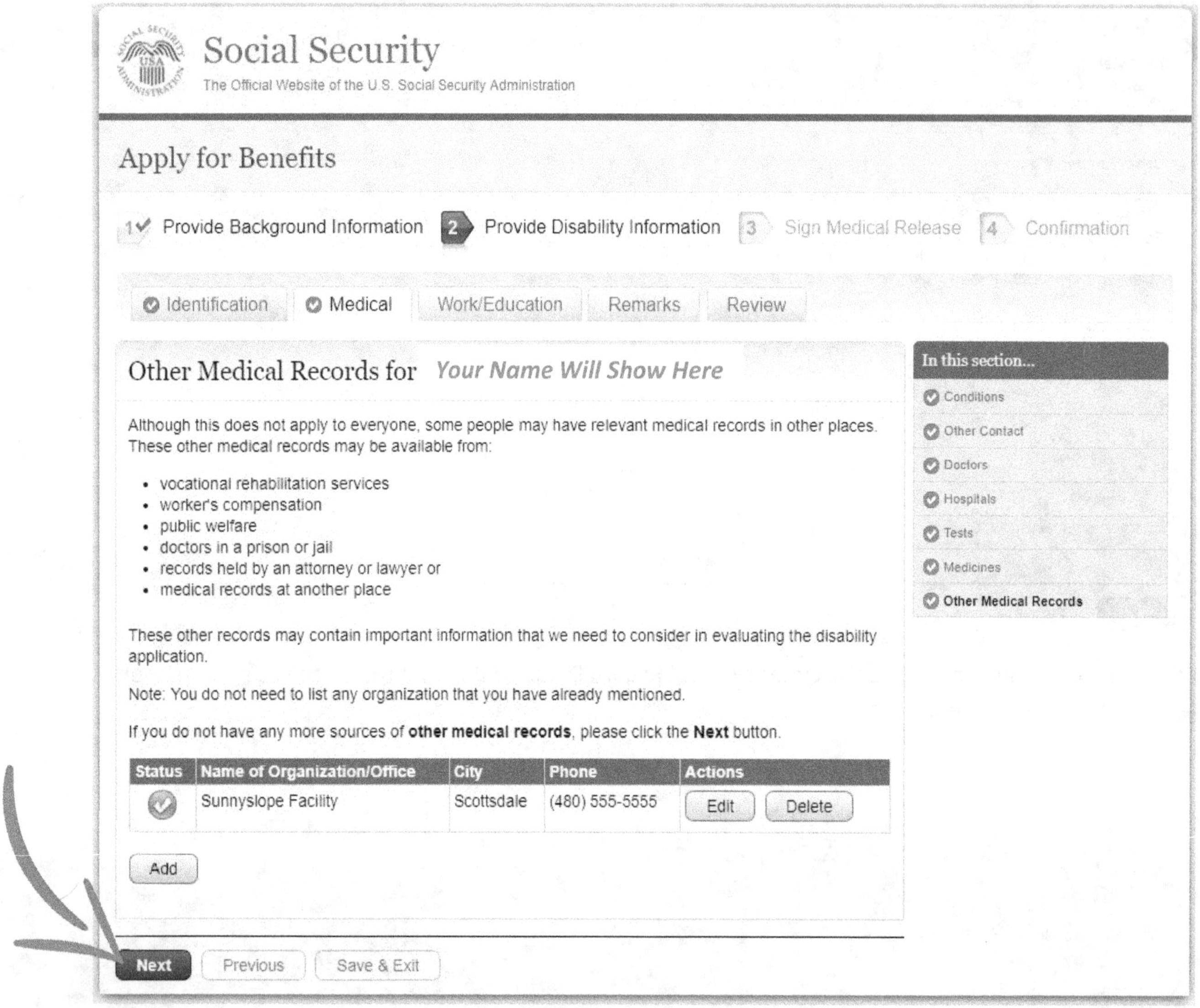

On this table, you'll see the Other Medical Record that you just added.

You can always click the "**Edit**" button to modify the Other Medical Record data or the "**Delete**" button to remove an Other Medical Record from the table.

Continue to add new Other Medical Records until you're finished.

Click the "**Next**" button to continue to the "Work/Education" section.

Need a break? By this point, you've probably been working on your application for at least two hours, and it may be a good time to click the "**Save & Exit**" button to rest your eyes and your brain. If you take a break now, you can review your information when you're feeling rested and your eyes are fresh, which will help you ensure the accuracy of your answers before moving on to the next section.

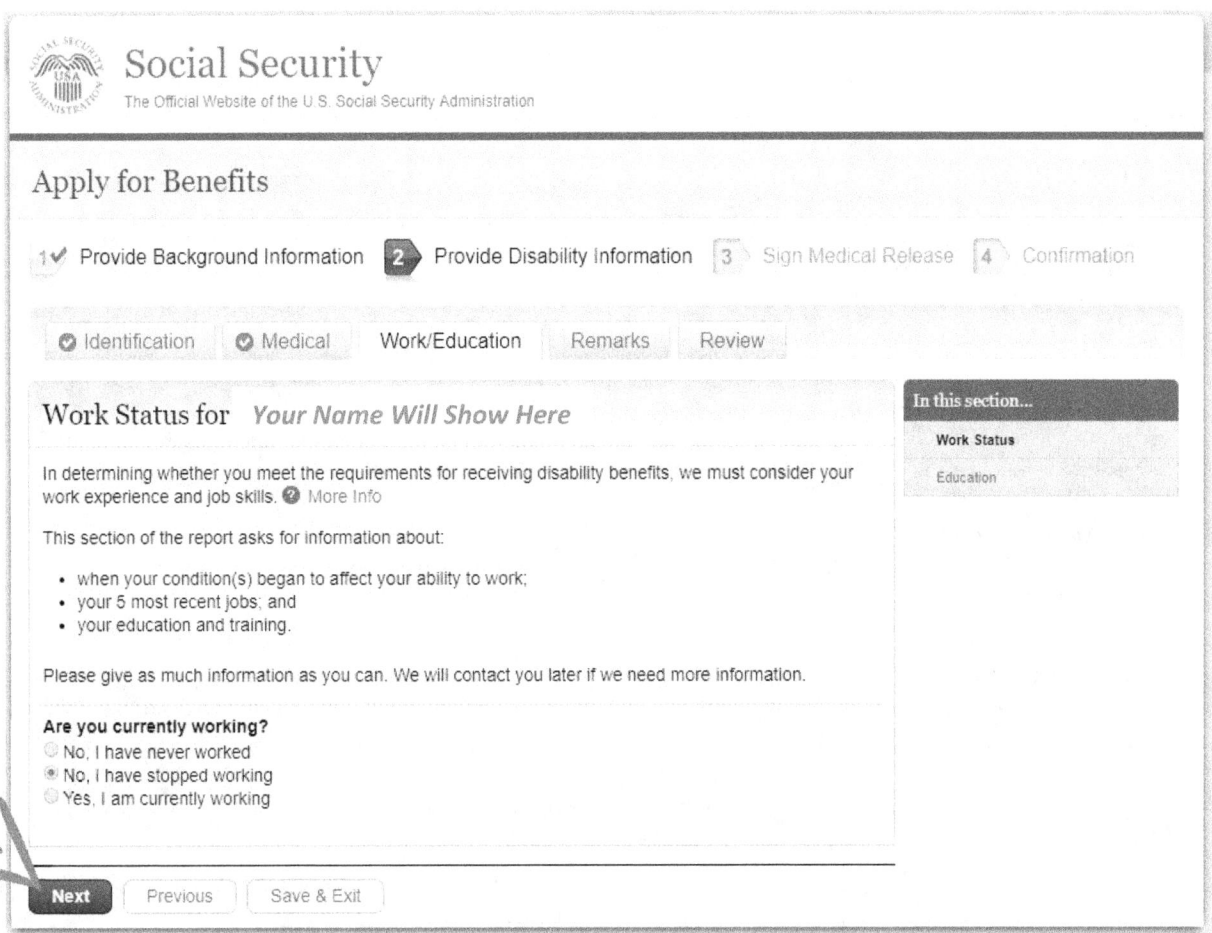

This screen is the beginning of the "Work/Education" section.

First, select the appropriate option for your current working status.

Click the "**Next**" button to continue to the "Work Activity" section.

On this page, indicate the date you stopped working (an approximate date based on memory will suffice).

Then Indicate why you stopped working.

Next, state whether your condition(s) caused you to make changes in your work activity before you stopped working.

If "**Yes**," indicate the exact or an approximate date you made changes to your work activity.

Click the "**Next**" button to continue to the "Job History" section.

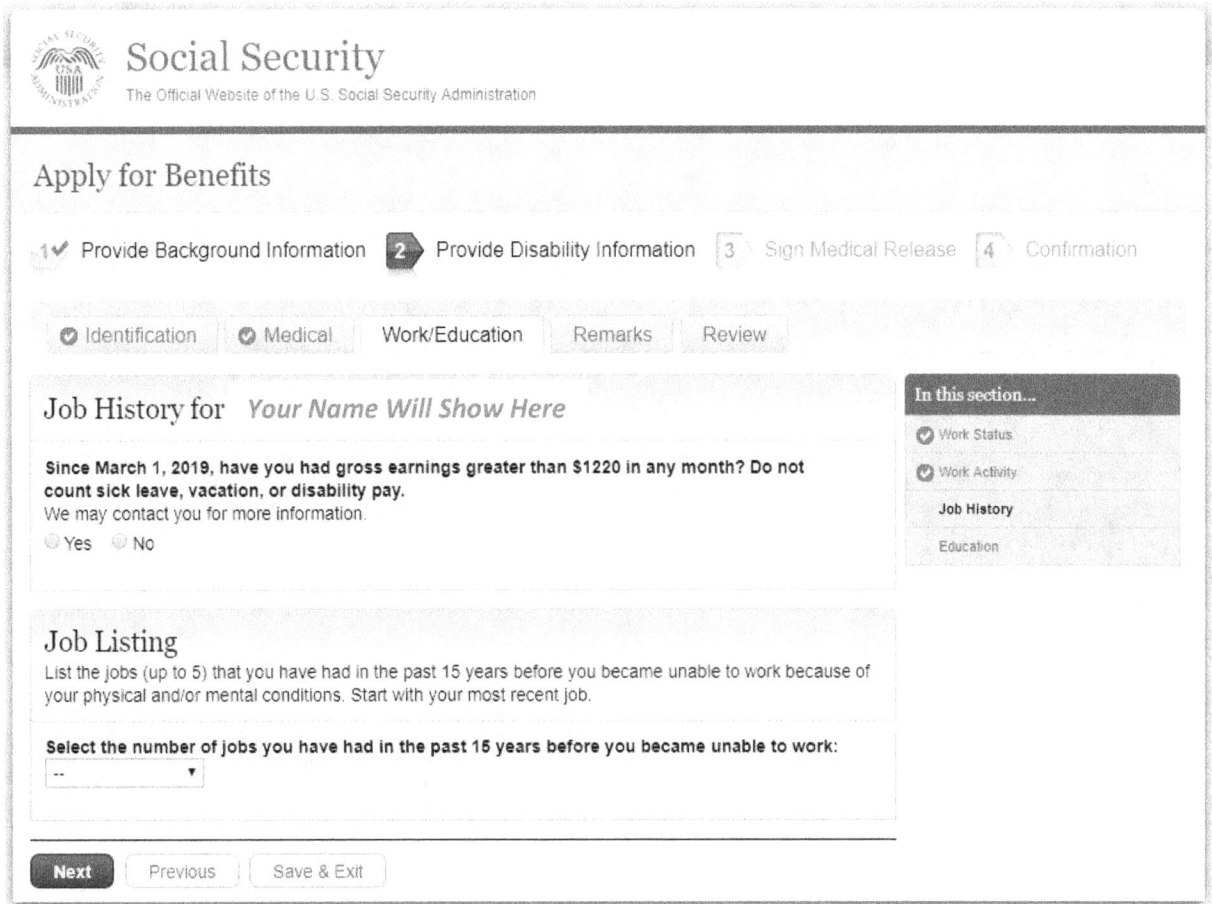

Here you'll indicate whether your gross earnings exceeded $1,220 in any month since the date you previously indicated that you stopped working.

Then select the number of jobs (up to 5) that you've held in the past 15 years, before you became unable to work because of your physical and/or mental condition(s).

Start with your most recent job and work backward.

Once you've select the number of jobs, you'll be asked to provide details about each job (see the next page).

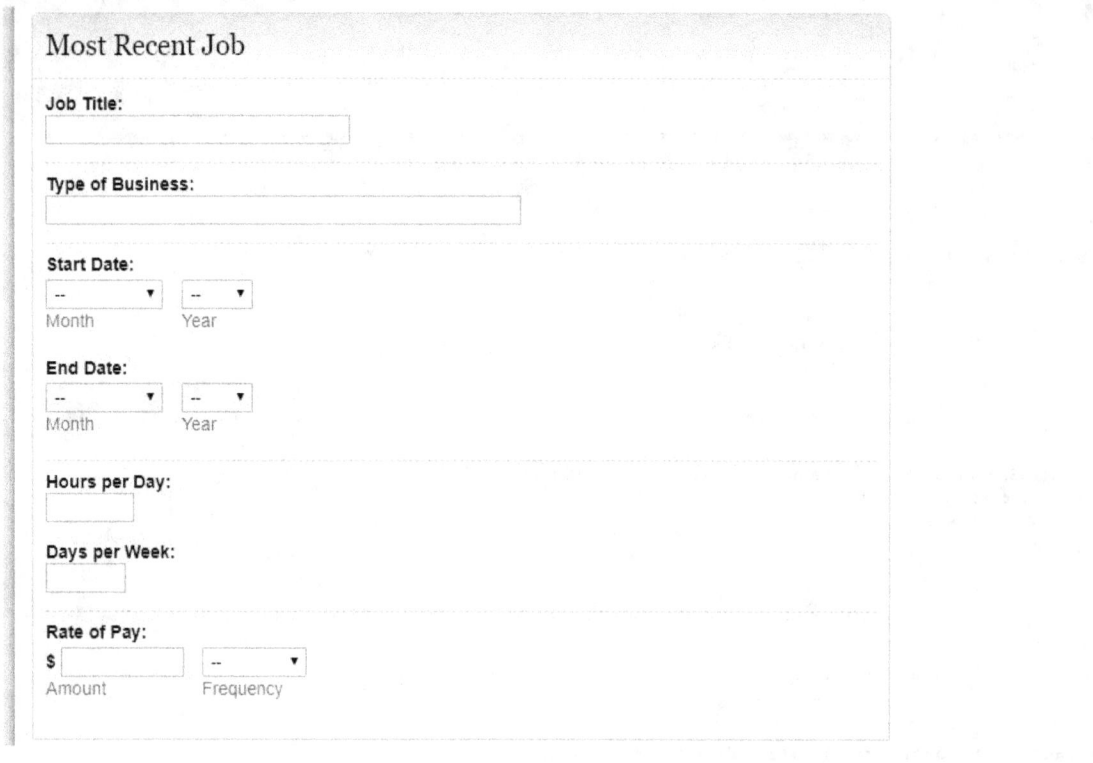

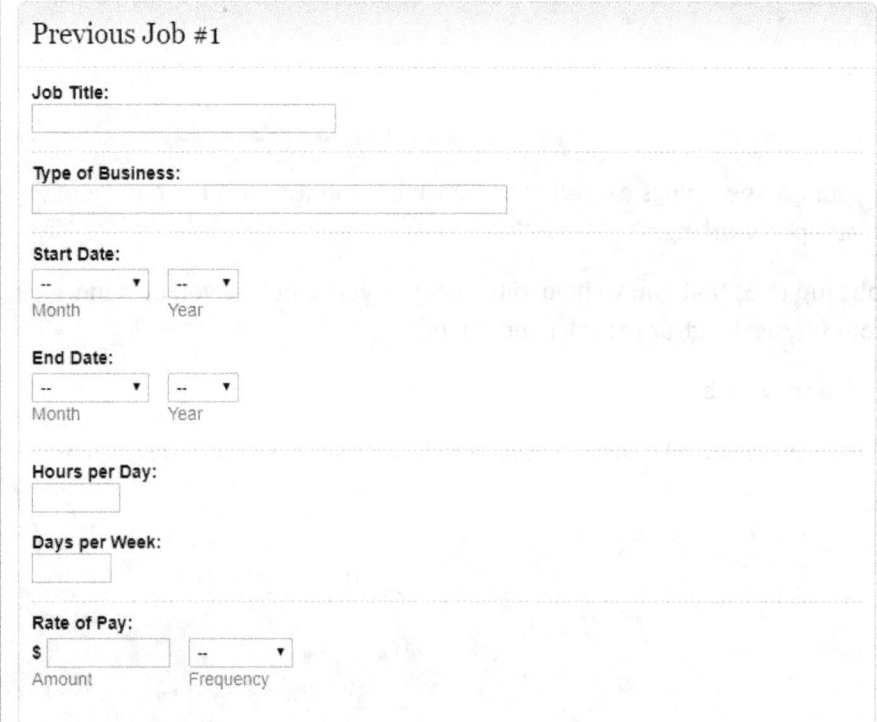

On this page, input all the details about your prior jobs, to the best of your ability.

Job Details (Part 1 of 2)

You may be asked to provide more detailed information about your past job(s):

Job Details

Describe this job: What did you do all day?
If you need more space, use the Remarks tab. (1000 characters maximum)

Characters remaining: 1000

In this job, did you use machines, tools, or equipment?
○ Yes ○ No

In this job, did you use technical knowledge or skills?
○ Yes ○ No

In this job, did you do any writing, complete reports, or perform any duties like this?
○ Yes ○ No

In this job, how many hours each day did you do each of the tasks listed below?
Do not include breaks and lunch.

Did you walk?
● Yes ○ No

How many hours did you walk?
[2 hours (Not very often) ▼]

Note: As you answer questions, a drop-down menu will pop up on the right side of the screen asking you to specify how many hours you were able to perform that type of activity.

Did you stand?
○ Yes ○ No

Did you sit?
○ Yes ○ No

Did you climb?
○ Yes ○ No

Did you stoop (bending down & forward at the waist?
○ Yes ○ No

Did you kneel (bending legs to rest on knees)?
○ Yes ○ No

Did you crouch (bending legs & back down & forward)?
○ Yes ○ No

Did you crawl?
○ Yes ○ No

Did you handle large objects?
○ Yes ○ No

Did you write, type or handle small objects?
○ Yes ○ No

Job Details (Part 2 of 2)

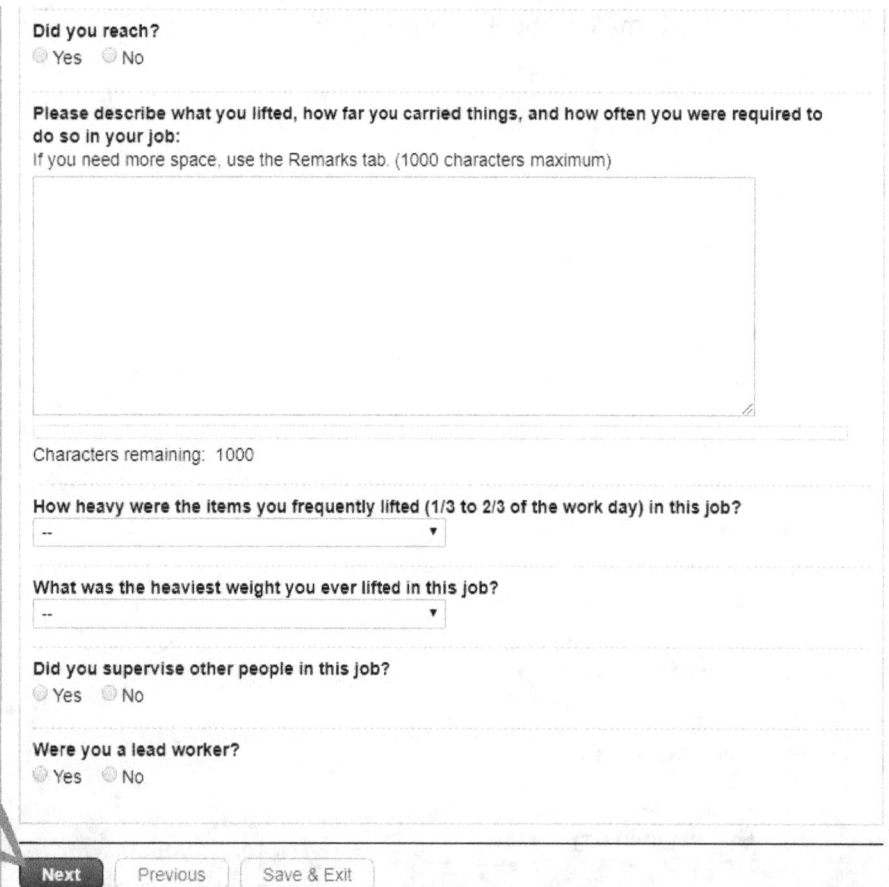

Note: I advise you to be very specific in your remarks in this section. Describe the different objects you carried and explain how far you carried them based on the approximate number of footsteps you took while holding the objects.

Continue to answer all questions regarding this job to the best of your knowledge.

Input information for all your jobs over the past 15 years.

Click the "**Next**" button to continue to the "Education and Training" section.

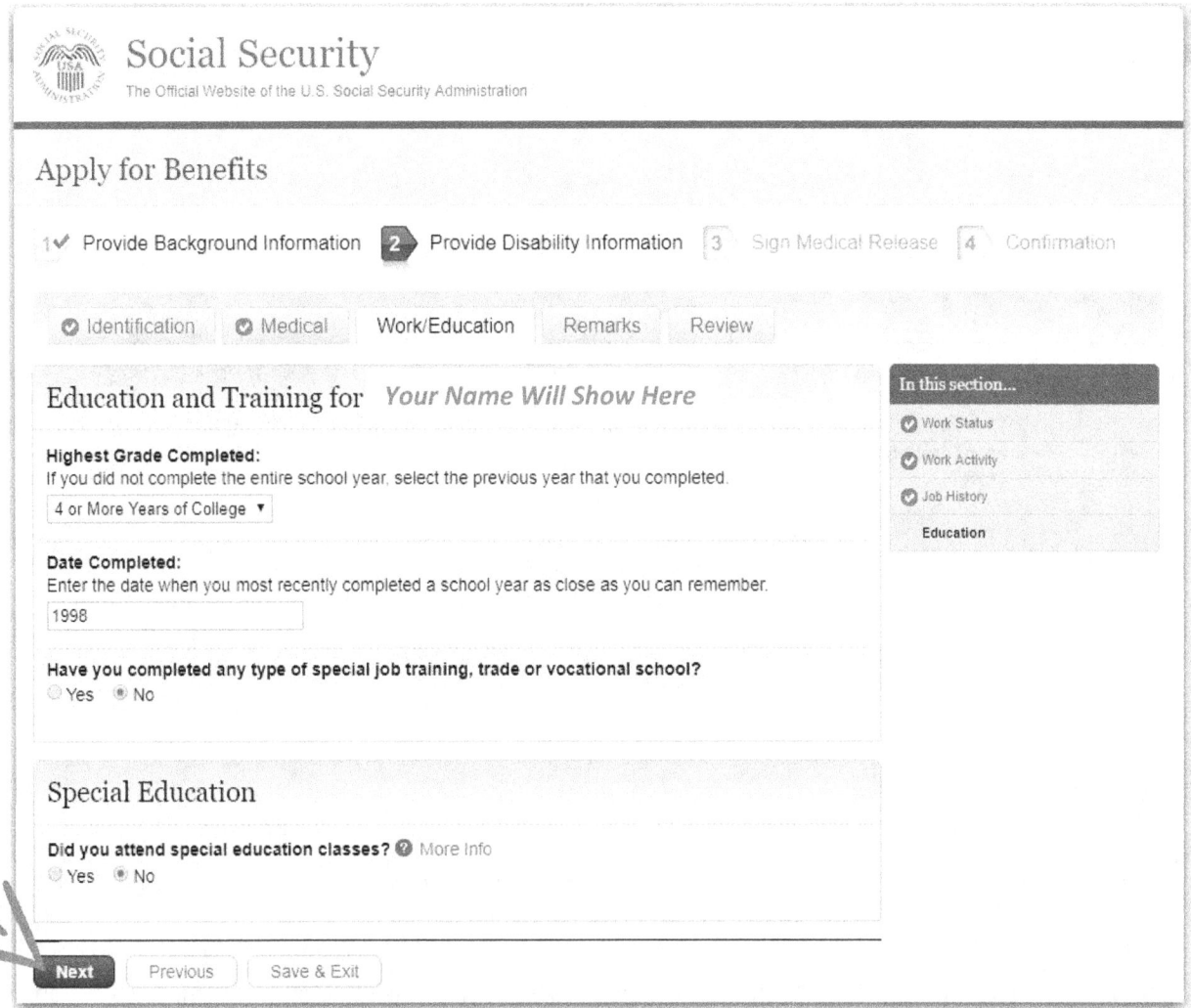

On this screen, input information pertaining to your Education and Training.

Select from the drop-down menu for the "**Highest Grade Completed**."

Then select the "**Date Completed**," even if it's just the month and the year or only the year.

Select whether you've completed any type of special job training or attended trade or vocational school.

If "**Yes**," input details.

Select whether you attended special education classes.

Click the "**Next**" button to continue to the "Remarks" section.

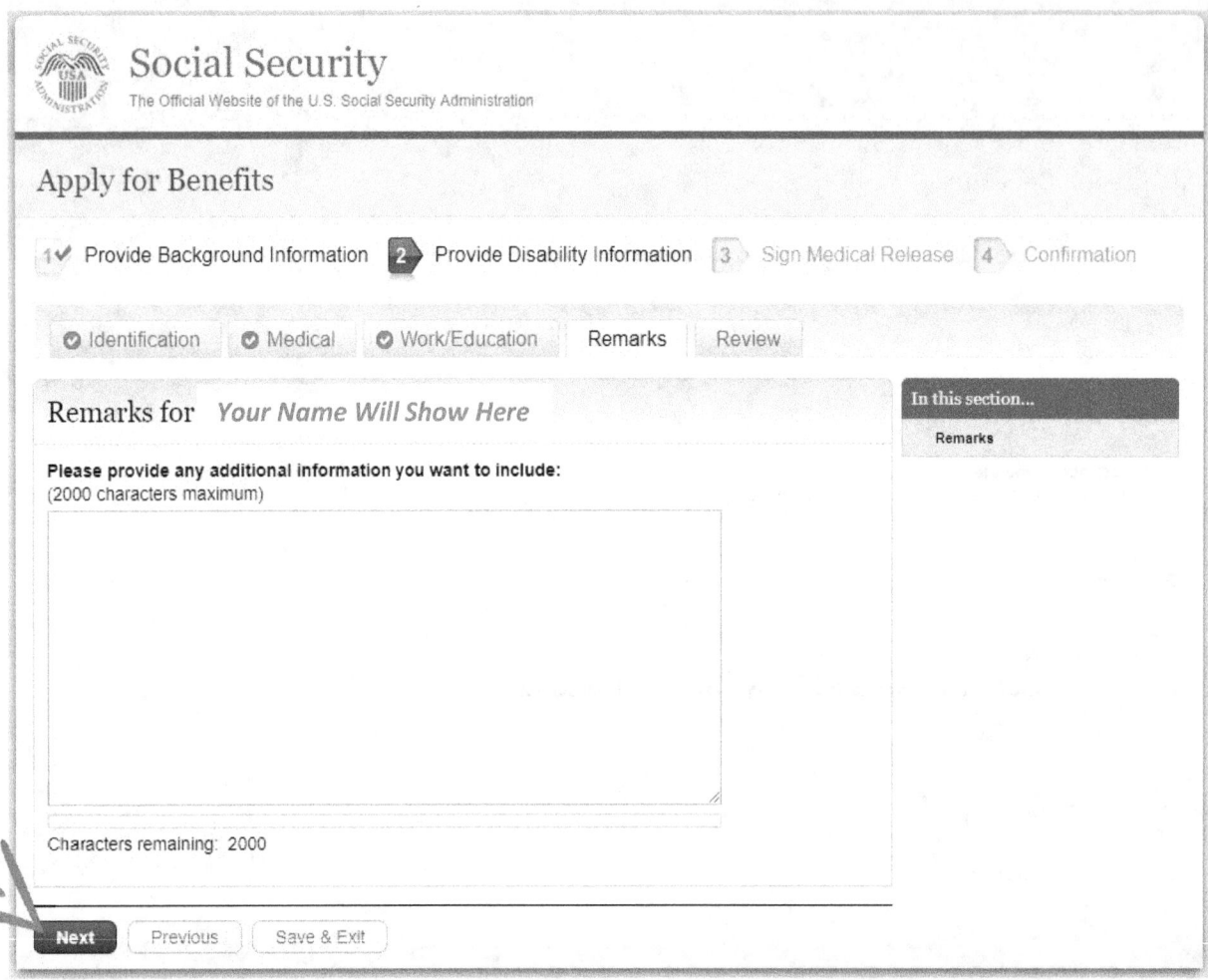

On this screen, you may input any "Remarks" or comments that you wish to include in your application. This is the perfect place to indicate that you're uncertain about any prior response. You can also use this space to let SSA know of any unique circumstances regarding your medical, work, or education history.

Click the "**Next**" button to review the information you provided in Step 2.

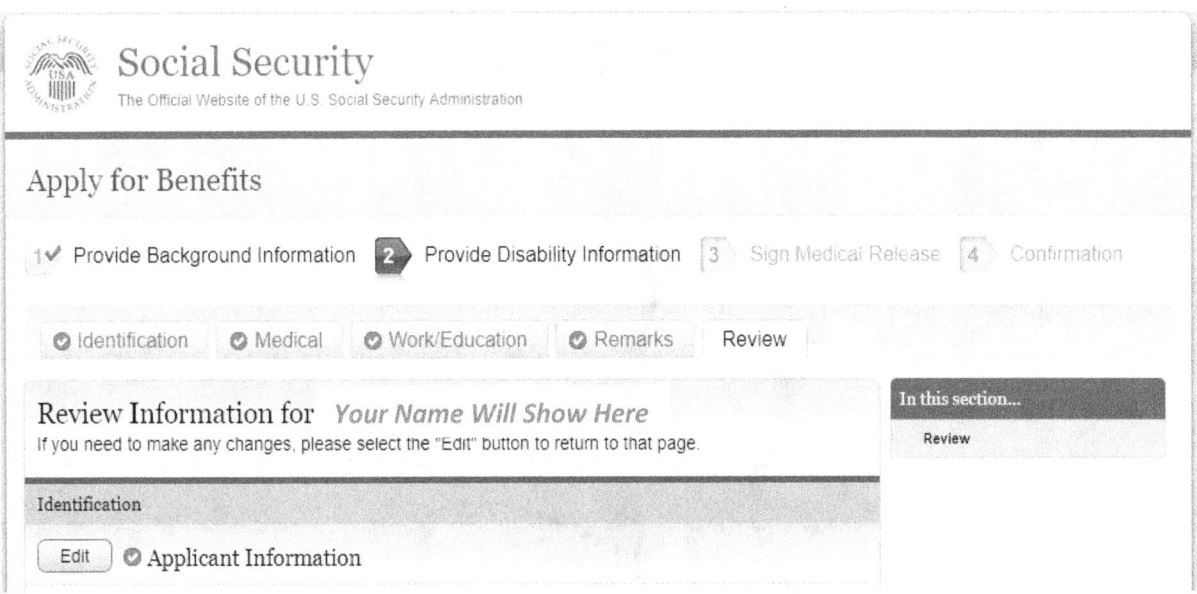

This page will display all the information you provided in the "Disability Information" section.

Review all information carefully. If you see any mistakes, you can click on the appropriate tab above to go backward into your application. You can also click on the "**Previous**" button at the bottom.

Once you've double-checked your information, you must review and accept the "**Electronic Signature Agreement**."

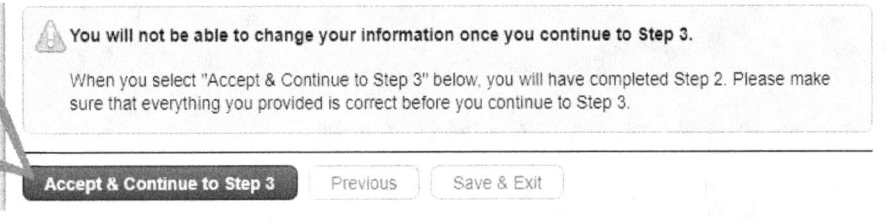

When ready, click the "**Accept & Continue**" button to proceed to Step 3.

Note: Once you click the "Accept & Continue" button, you won't be able to make any changes to your responses in Step 2. So it's very important that you answer questions truthfully and to the best of your ability before proceeding.

Excellent!

You've finished Step 2 of 4 of the application process.

You're now on Step 3.

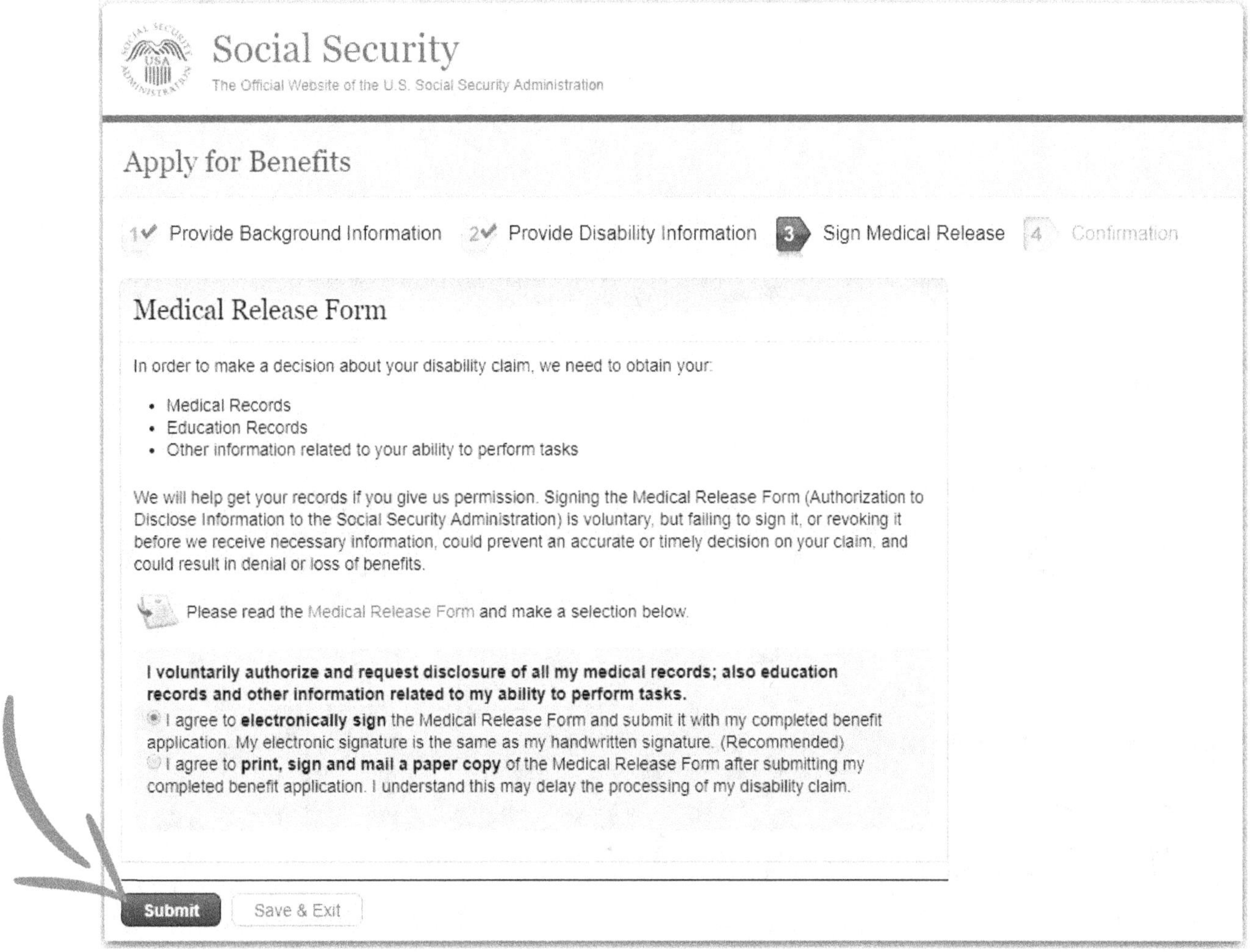

On Step 3, you'll be required to sign a Medical Release for SSA.

Indicate whether you prefer to "**electronically sign**" or to "**print, sign and mail a paper copy**" to SSA.

Note: If you indicate that you prefer to "**print, sign and mail a paper copy**," you'll see this message:

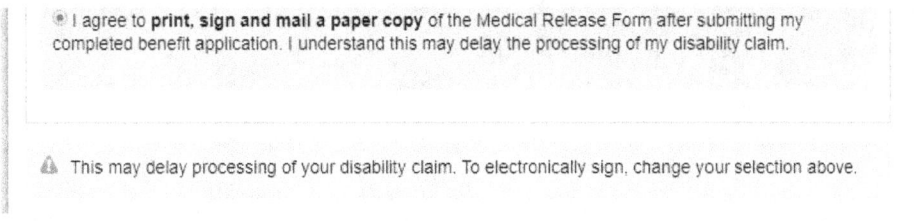

For fastest handling of your application, select the "**electronically sign**" option.

Click the "**Submit**" button to continue to Step 4.

Apply for Benefits

1. ✓ Provide Background Information 2. ✓ Provide Disability Information 3. ✓ Sign Medical Release **4. Confirmation**

  Thank you for applying for disability online.

Your Confirmation Number is: **89122274**   ← Save this number for your records.

You can check the status of your application online by signing into or creating a *my* Social Security account.

We will contact you with any updates or questions we may have about your information.

What you need to do next: ← These are the remaining action steps needed to complete your filing.

1. **Gather** the following documents:
   - Any medical evidence you already have about your disability;
   - Award letters, pay stubs, settlement agreements or other proof of temporary or permanent workers' compensation type benefits you received.
2. **Print and sign** medical release form;
3. **Print** your personalized cover sheet;
4. **Mail** all of these items to:
   SOCIAL SECURITY
   16241 N TATUM BLVD   ← This is the local SSA field office that will be processing your claim.
   PHOENIX, AZ 85032-3441

If you prefer to bring your documents in person, you can visit **your** local **Social Security office**.

If you do not have all the documents listed above we will help you get any documents you need.

Caution: Do not mail foreign records or any Department of Homeland Security (DHS) documents to us - especially those you are required to keep with you at all times. These documents are sensitive and expensive to replace if lost; and some cannot be replaced. Instead, **bring them to your** local **Social Security office** where they will be examined and returned to you.

🖨 Print this page

View and Print Your Receipt ← Click this link to print or save a copy of your receipt.
We recommend that you keep a copy for your records.

We May Need Additional Documents

Please gather the following document(s) and keep them in a convenient place so you will have them ready when you are contacted by a Social Security representative:

- Wages from your employer for last year (e.g., copy of your W-2 form). We can accept a photocopy of this document.
- Self-employment income for last year (e.g., IRS Schedules C and SE). We can accept a photocopy of these documents.

Useful Links | Contact Us

- Reporting Responsibilities: What Needs to be Reported
- Frequently Asked Questions - Internet Benefit Claim
- Social Security Online: What You Can Do Online
- Voluntary Tax Withholding
- Helpful Health Information Online
- Prescription Assistance

[Done]

You've finished the online filing process!

Once you've completed the remaining action steps highlighted on the confirmation screen, your application for disability benefits will be reviewed by your local SSA field office.

Some important things to keep in mind:

(1)

Don't delay in sending in the remaining documents.

This includes medical evidence, the signed medical release form, and the cover letter.

The sooner you get the documents in, the sooner your application will be reviewed!

(2)

Save the confirmation number and other data in a safe place.

Print out a copy of your completed application and save the confirmation number for your records.

What Happens Next?

Initial Application:

Now that your application for Social Security disability benefits has been filed, your local SSA field office will review it. First, there will be a preliminary review of your application and your Social Security statement. This preliminary review is largely automated. A software program that is proprietary to the Social Security Administration will check several factors on your application and generate a findings summary.

Then a claims handler will review the findings summary along with the information you provided in your application. Once SSA is in receipt of a signed medical release (Form SSA-827), SSA will request your medical records from your doctors. After receiving your records, your claims handler will review them to see if you have a severe diagnosis and if the disability or condition meets one of the "listings."

Electronic applications can take between 10 and 16 weeks to process. According to a 2010 report published by the SSA*, **approximately 36.3% of initial applications are approved**. It's worth noting that in 2000, approximately 40.8% of initial applications were approved. It appears that the percentage of initial application approvals is declining each year.

Request for Reconsideration:

If your application for disability benefits is denied, you'll have approximately 65 days from the date shown on your denial letter to file a **request for reconsideration**. This is a low-level appeal at the field office that decided your initial claim. A request for reconsideration may also be filed electronically on www.ssa.gov, which can take between 4 and 12 weeks to process. The processing time may vary, depending on the amount of additional medical evidence the field office must review.

According to the same 2010 report published by the SSA*, **approximately 8.1% of reconsiderations are approved** (overturning the initial denial).

Request for a Hearing with an Administrative Law Judge (ALJ):

If your reconsideration request is denied, you'll have approximately 65 days from the date shown on your denial letter to request a hearing before an Administrative Law Judge. This is the stage in the process where most claims are awarded.

According to the same 2010 report published by the SSA*, **approximately 76.1% of medical decisions at the hearing level are approved**.

*See: https://www.ssa.gov/policy/docs/statcomps/di_asr/2011/sect04.html

When Should You Consider Hiring an Attorney Representative?

Here are the published statistics on the approval rate at the various stages of the disability claim review process:

Initial filings:	36%
Reconsideration requests:	8%
Hearing with a judge:	76%

An overwhelming majority of successful claims are awarded at the hearing level. This is largely because most claimants are represented at a hearing by an attorney or a non-attorney representative.

If your initial application is denied, you should strongly consider consulting with an attorney who can review your claim. An attorney with experience can evaluate your claim and provide you with a candid assessment. This information is extremely important and helpful because your life may be on "pause" pending the outcome of your claim.

Since you're not working, or working minimally, you may be experiencing hardship. If a Social Security disability attorney accepts your case, your attorney will ensure that all required forms, appeals, and requests are properly filed, and that your best available medical evidence is highlighted, thereby increasing the odds of a swift and successful review of your disability claim. Due to the multitude of nuances in the claims review process, an attorney with experience will be able to formulate a solid legal theory that demonstrates to the SSA that you're totally disabled and that you're legally entitled to receive Social Security benefits.

Overview of Social Security Disability Insurance "SSDI"

To qualify for Social Security Disability Insurance benefits, an individual must be completely disabled according to the Social Security Administration's ("SSA") definition of total disability. That individual must also be eligible for SSDI, that is, the individual has worked and paid Federal Insurance Contributions Act (FICA) premiums at least 5 of the past 10 years. In most cases, if you have worked for an outside employer in the United States, you have made FICA contributions (as has your employer).

> *Definition of disability: applicant must not be able to engage in any substantial gainful activity because of a medically-determinable physical or mental impairment(s) that is expected to result in death or has lasted or is expected to last for a continuous period of at least 12 months.*

To qualify for total disability, an individual must be completely unable to perform any work which he/she has performed in the past. It is critically important to have objective medical evidence to prove to SSA that the individual is in fact disabled. That is why it is very important to continue seeing a doctor or specialist regularly.

Having a medical record demonstrating one or more of these disabilities, conditions, or impairments will help your claim for social security disability benefits. Here are some of the more commonly included medical conditions:

- Heart conditions
- Digestive disorders
- Thyroid disorders
- Blood disorders
- Immune system disorders
- Hearing or vision loss
- Mental conditions and disorders
- Neck, back, and spine injuries
- Neurological problems
- Lung infections and Asthma
- Skin disorders
- Multiple body system impairments

For the complete "Listing of Impairments", you can visit:
https://www.ssa.gov/disability/professionals/bluebook/AdultListings.htm

Overview of Supplemental Security Income "SSI"

The SSI program pays benefits to disabled adults and children who have limited income and resources. Also, SSI benefits are payable to people 65 and older without disabilities who meet the financial limits. People who have worked long enough may also be able to receive Social Security disability or retirement benefits as well as SSI.

For most people, the medical requirements for disability payments are the same under both SSD and SSI and disability is determined by the same process. Whether you apply for Social Security or SSI disability, you will be asked to provide information about your medical condition, work and education history to help the Social Security Administration decide if you are disabled under their rules.

Common Questions

As an attorney practicing social security disability law, I receive a wide variety of questions about disability law. I've compiled some of the more common questions that I get asked in this section.

Q: How long must I wait after becoming disabled before filing for disability benefits?

A: Not another moment! In fact, you file for disability benefits on the very same day that you become disabled. Many folks make the unfortunate mistake of waiting months or even years after becoming disabled before filing a Social Security disability claim. The best advice is to consult with an attorney immediately.

Q: I got hurt on the job and I am collecting workers' compensation benefits. Can I also file a claim for Social Security disability benefits now?

A: Absolutely! You do not have to wait until the worker's compensation ends. An individual can file a claim for Social Security disability benefits while receiving workers' compensation benefits. In fact, it is recommended to file the Social Security disability claim as soon as possible to avoid any gap between when the workers' compensation is finished, and the Social Security disability benefits begin.

Q: How do I know if I will be found disabled by Social Security?

A: Don't overthink it! If you feel as though you cannot seek gainful employment because of an injury or disability, you should absolutely file a claim for benefits. Why wouldn't you? That is why the money is there in the first place. Many good claims get denied regularly, so don't be discouraged if the initial claim is denied. If denied, you should consult with an experienced attorney to get an opinion as to the chances of success on appeal.

Q: Do you have to be permanently disabled to get Social Security disability benefits?

A: No. You have to have been disabled for at least a year or be expected to be disabled for at least a year or have a condition that can be expected to result in death within a year.

Q: I have several health problems, but no one of them disables me. It is the combination that disables me. Can I get Social Security disability benefits?

A: Maybe. Social Security ought to consider the combination of conditions or impairments that an individual suffers in determining disability (can gainful employment be sought?). Many, perhaps most claimants for Social Security disability benefits have more than one health problem and the combined effects of all of the health problems must be considered.

Q: I got hurt in car accident. I am disabled now, but I intend to return to work after I recover. Should I file for Social Security disability benefits?

A: It's not a bad idea to file! If you believe there is a decent chance you'll be out of work for a year or more you should definitely file for Social Security disability benefits.

Q: How does Social Security determine if I am disabled?

A: Good question. When your claim is being examined, the Social Security Administration will review your medical records. Further, other facts will be considered such as all your health problems, your age, education, and work experience. Generally, Social Security is supposed to decide whether you can do your past work. If Social Security decides that you are unable to do your past work, they will then consider whether there is any other work (theoretical employment) which you can do considering your health problems and your age, education, and work experience.

Created by Jeffrey R. Herman
Social Security Disability Attorney

Social Security Disability Benefits Initial Filing Guide
Copyright 2019 Law Office of Jeffrey Herman, PLC
All Rights Reserved

7272 E. Indian School Rd. Suite 540
Scottsdale, AZ 85251
Ph: (844) 454-3762

jeffrey@jhermanlaw.com

www.ingramcontent.com/pod-product-compliance
Lightning Source LLC
Chambersburg PA
CBHW081012170526
45158CB00010B/3009